KATA & TOR

Also by Kevin Crossley-Holland

Arthur: The Always King

Between Worlds: Folktales of Britain & Ireland

King Alfred and the Ice Coffin

Norse Myths: Tales of Odin, Thor and Loki

Norse Tales: Stories of Odin and Loki on Middle Earth

KATA & TOR

KEVIN CROSSLEY-HOLLAND

This is a work of fiction. Names, characters, places and incidents are either the product of the author's imagination or, if real, used fictitiously. All statements, activities, stunts, descriptions, information and material of any other kind contained herein are included for entertainment purposes only and should not be relied on for accuracy or replicated as they may result in injury.

First published 2025 by Walker Books Ltd
87 Vauxhall Walk, London SE11 5HJ

2 4 6 8 10 9 7 5 3 1

Text © 2025 Kevin Crossley-Holland
Cover illustration © 2025 Daniel Burgess

The right of Kevin Crossley-Holland to be identified as author of this work has been asserted in accordance with the Copyright, Designs and Patents Act 1988

EU Authorized Representative: HackettFlynn Ltd, 36 Cloch Choirneal, Balrothery, Co. Dublin, K32 C942, Ireland. EU@walkerpublishinggroup.com

This book has been typeset in Berkeley Oldstyle

Printed and bound by CPI Group (UK) Ltd, Croydon CR0 4YY

All rights reserved. No part of this book may be reproduced, transmitted or stored in an information retrieval system in any form or by any means, graphic, electronic or mechanical, including photocopying, taping and recording, without prior written permission from the publisher.

British Library Cataloguing in Publication Data:
a catalogue record for this book is available from the British Library

ISBN 978-1-4063-9905-9

www.walker.co.uk

For
Lynda Edwardes-Evans
with love and gratitude

CHARACTER LIST

Tor, Norwegian, aged fifteen (King Harald Hardrada's illegitimate third son)
Kata, English, aged fifteen (a villager of Riccall)

Villagers of Riccall

Wilf (the village headman)
Father Huw (the village priest)
Bullfrog (the owner of the watermill)
Puttnam (a reed-cutter)
Eager, aged six (his son)
Isen, aged five (Eager's brother)
Borden (a blacksmith)
Ellette (his young wife)
Bliss, aged three (their daughter)
May (Borden's sister)
Kendra (a wise woman)
Oswald, aged sixteen (a young villager)
Edith (Kata's mother, deceased)
Mattie (a village woman)
Hilda, aged fifteen (Mattie's daughter)
Odda (a young villager)
Orva (a fisher girl and Odda's twin sister)
Rinan (a fisherman)
Snell (a fisherman)

Vikings

Harald Hardrada (King of Norway)
Ellisif (wife of Harald Hardrada and Queen of Norway)
Magnus (their first son and regent)
Young Olaf (their second son)
Maria (their daughter)
Saint Olaf (King Harald's dead half-brother and patron saint of Norway)
Thjodolf (a skald)
Arnor (a skald)
Fridrek (King Harald's banner-bearer)
Orri Eystein (a young Norwegian leader)
Eirik (a scout)
Bard (Eirik's brother, also a scout)
Arni (a scout)
Solveig (Tor's mother)

Anglo-Saxons and Others

Harold Godwinson (King of England)
Tostig (his brother and the deposed Earl of Northumbria)
Morcar (Earl of Northumbria)
Edwin (Morcar's elder brother and Earl of Mercia)
Bridget (Mother Superior of the nunnery in York)
Innocenta (a young Irish sister at the nunnery)
Matason (skipper of *Mævill*, a trading boat)
Safae (Matason's Sicilian ship-wife)
Razon (a Moorish slave)
Mundir (a Moorish slave)

With shields overlapping along their bulwarks,
three hundred warships surged-and-sang
in sunlight and in the moon-glade gleamed.
Never was such a fleet assembled
in Norway, or anywhere on Middle Earth.
Waverer and Neigher and Roaming Traveller
filled our canvas, and standing beside
his dragon prow, our old king proclaimed:
"I sail in the name of my own birthright.
I sail south to lay claim in England."

CHAPTER 1

Tor crouched on all fours.

He tried to tighten the muscles in his neck, his strong shoulders, his forearms, his whole body. He felt so cold. Freezing. He kept shaking and shuddering as if his entire being were tearing itself to pieces. As soon as he tried to take a deep breath he started to cough.

The sharp gravel bit into his raw palms and knees, drawing blood.

Above him, the sun throbbed behind dark clouds. Ravens croaked and whirled; a sea eagle shrieked.

Tor bowed his head.

When at last he felt able to look around, what was there to see? The grey German Ocean, not flat-calm because it never is, quite good-humoured though: soft-ribbed, darted with pewter sparks. And to north and south, the stretch of the barren foreshore and long line of jagged, dark cliffs.

So, this was England. Uninviting. Desolate.

It looks like the world's end, thought Tor, if the world does end.

But when he narrowed his eyes again, Tor did see something. A lump lying on the beach.

He got to his feet, dripping, and staggered towards it. Sobbing, he fell onto his knees.

The late sun burst through the lumpen clouds and thumped inside his head.

Tor knew. He knew for sure.

"Eirik!"

Eirik, self-reliant and strong. His arms and legs broken and twisted when the sea chewed him before she threw him up. His white, unblemished skin. His grey eyes, open and amazed. The sand flies exploring his nostrils and ears and gaping mouth. And a ribbon of seaweed had draped itself around his neck and shoulders, as if he were a bridegroom of the sea.

Eirik, Tor's friend and companion in a land of strangers.

I'm alone in an enemy country, Tor thought. I don't even know where I am.

Tor howled and threw himself over Eirik's mangled body.

"Eirik, Eirik." Tor's lips were bluish with cold. He was mouthing the words but made scarcely a sound.

When at last Tor levered himself up, he saw their boat floating in the wavelets, her bow ribs broken, her pine mast snapped, her square sail lying flat in the water.

Kittiwake… Kittiwake… What happened?

The wind was from the north, like she was all the way from Orkney. Right behind us from the hour we set sail.

What happened?

One moment, we were surging forward, the next we collided. Not ice. It can't have been, not this far south.

A whale?

It couldn't have been the whirlpool, he thought. That's much further north, unless there is a second one. Swimming ghosts? No, they wouldn't capsize my *Kittiwake*. She'd sail straight through them.

Tor stumbled out to *Kittiwake*, and at once he saw how badly damaged she was. Wrecked. Good for nothing but driftwood.

The ocean glittered. The shadow of a dark cloud advanced towards him over the offing.

It's Ran, thought Tor. The goddess of the sea. She's down there with her drowning net, gloating over her victim. How ever many of us she drowns, she always wants more, more.

But not only had Ran spared Tor; she had spared his sea coat as well. A great, bulky mass of a thing, coarsely woven and thickly lined, and smeared all over with pig's fat. He'd thrown it off so he could swim, but Eirik, poor Eirik, he hadn't known how to swim.

The coat was bobbing up and down on the far side of *Kittiwake*, and Tor waded round and grabbed it. For all his strong shoulders, it was so drenched and heavy he had to drag it behind him.

Then Tor splashed back to his dead companion. He shuddered. He reached down, closed his friend's eyes, and pulled away the slimy seaweed that had wrapped around his neck.

Tor knew he must bury him so he could begin his journey to the next world.

Where, though? And what could he dig with?

What if the tide turns and tugs at him? thought Tor.

He trembled, and simply slumped beside his dead friend's body. He didn't know how to begin.

When Tor at last opened his eyes, the light was so bright he squeezed his eyelids tightly shut again. He didn't want to face the day.

Behind his closed lids, Tor saw his own father, King Harald Hardrada, a full head taller than he was, turning towards him with his bright blue eyes, and Tor was back in Trondheim in Norway, and it was midsummer.

"Your role is crucial," the king had told him. "Now's almost the time for me to invade England. I want you to be my leading scout. To travel ahead, nose around, find out everything you can. But wait for us when you reach Scarborough. That's where I mean to lay up with my fleet and take stock."

Tor nodded.

"Check the best landfalls," said the king. "Merchants have often told me how dangerous the coast is. Dark cliffs. Submerged rocks. I'll send Eirik with you. Whatever you do, keep together. Scouts always work in pairs."

How can we do that now! thought Tor. Eirik, you've deserted me. And how can I scout the land? I don't even know where I am.

Tor felt so very tired.

His head hurt, and he couldn't think straight. He pressed his right hand over his heart to stop it from bursting.

After some time, Tor got to his feet, and at once staggered sideways. He forced himself upright. He knew he must bury Eirik. It was no good putting it off. He grabbed his companion's hands and slowly hauled him a little way. But it was too much. Eirik was too heavy.

I'll find some food, Tor thought. I'm so hungry. Then I'll come back and bury him.

On his own, Tor walked further up the beach. At the foot of the high cliffs, he found a tumbledown shack. He reached for the frame of the door, and for a moment he was nervous. What if someone is inside? No, Tor, he told himself. I'm a Viking. We don't feel fear.

"Anyone there?" he barked. "Anyone?"

The shack was empty.

Then he heaved his drenched sea coat up onto the curved roof and hung it over two wooden pegs to dry.

The smell inside the shack was overpowering – sea salt and pitch and rotting seaweed, dead fish, sweat, excrement.

The little fireplace in the middle of the room was lifeless. Beside it, in two small clay pots, there was some drinking water and a dozen berries. He stooped, swilled down the sour water and crammed the berries into his mouth.

As his eyes became more used to the gloom, Tor made out, in one corner, a whole mound of marsh plants, sea sage and thrift, aster and sea lavender.

A bed, thought Tor. A bed! Someone has been here recently. They might come back at any time. But I'm so tired. I don't care.

Eirik. Eirik. I'll come back to bury you.

And that's all he thought. He took a deep breath and collapsed into the bed.

There were several cracks between the ash planks in the low roof and, although they had been stuffed with seaweed and mud, they kept opening again like wounds that refused to heal.

The sun spied sleeping Tor through one of these fissures. It dazzled him, and Tor sat up with a jerk, as if he expected to be attacked. But when he'd had a good look around, he could see that his only companion was a noisy fly.

Outside the door, a gull was sounding impatient. It poked its head into the cabin and croaked insistently.

"Clear off!" Tor told it. And at once he heard how the sea salt had almost taken away his voice.

At least I've got a voice, he thought. A husky one. I've got a tongue. And I know how to use it.

Tor's quick wits were partly why his father had chosen him as a scout. "Your craftiness," King Harald had told him. "The way you make things up."

Well, at least I'm some use to him, thought Tor. I mean, I haven't got a steady hand like Magnus; he'll be a good ruler while my father's away in England. And I'll never be agile or eager in battle, like my other half-brother, Young Olaf. How could I be? I've never been trained to fight, living away on the farm with my mother.

The first thing Tor saw when he stepped outside was how high the sun had already climbed. Halfway up to the zenith.

I never sleep this long, he thought. Not since I was little.

The second was that the shack was really half of an upside-down boat. The back half of a coble, upended.

Clinker, he thought. The same as *Kittiwake*. But this one has a flat bottom. He ran his left hand along one of the planks. Maybe she was wrecked, too and dragged up under this cliff.

The third thing Tor saw was his sea coat, still pegged to the roof. It was gently steaming as it dried out. When he reached up and smoothed it with both hands, Tor immediately felt a lump inside it – something sewn into the bottom corner of the lining.

The walrus ivory box containing his uncle's, Saint Olaf's, toenail.

Tor remembered standing with his father outside the little chapel in Trondheim. The warden had been waiting for them, and he had pulled out a large key from inside his leather breeches and unlocked the door.

The king had crossed over the clay tiles of the chapel floor to the north wall, where a little bucket was tied with a rope to an iron ring in the wall, and they had both washed their hands in the gleaming, cold spring water in the bucket before approaching the altar.

The moment Tor saw the silver-gilt casket that contained his uncle, Tor caught his breath. His father opened the lid and Tor stared down at Saint Olaf's corpse, so peaceful, so sweet-smelling, so lily-like. Harald stroked Saint Olaf's eyebrows, and then, with the little pair of silver scissors lying at Olaf's side, cut the saint's fingernails, one by one. They were black now, and glossy and hard. "For a long time, they kept growing," Harald said, turning to his son. "Cut one of his toenails," he told him quietly.

Tor frowned and swept back his long, fair hair. He didn't want to touch the body of his uncle.

"Go on!" the king said.

So Tor screwed up his face and cut one nail – a little one.

"Keep it safe," King Harald said. "Keep it safe, my son, and it will keep you safe. It will protect you. You could ask your mother to carve a walrus ivory box to house it, so you can always carry it with you."

With his teeth, Tor pulled at the lining of his sea coat. Then he grasped the little walrus ivory box and carefully unlatched the lid.

Standing in the sunlight outside the coble, Tor stared for a while at the toenail in its wad of bog-cotton, and somehow the sight of it strengthened his mind and his resolve to do what had to be done. Then Tor stuffed the nail underneath the bog-cotton, shut and latched the lid of the box, and slid it back inside the lining of his sea coat.

It was time to bury his friend.

CHAPTER 2

Kata ground the blade of her sickle with a wedge of whetstone and gazed down her long acre again. The field mouse that had been carefully watching her from its nest made a run for it. It bolted straight over the grass ridge into the next acre, only for Oswald to crush its delicate skull with the flat of a spade.

"Thirteen!" yelled Oswald.

Kata took a deep breath, and slowly expelled it. And Oswald's the best of the bunch, she thought. The other Riccall boys are coarse and boring. Lumps and loaves.

"Yah!" yelled Oswald as he lunged at another field mouse, but he missed it.

Kata stooped again, and the sickle twisted between her hands. Her back ached and her hands were red and sore. It was such hard work she had little time to daydream, but just now and then a memory made her shiver or smile.

She saw herself hiding in a nest of ripe wheat when she was a little girl; her mother, Edith, swinging her sickle right above her and laughing. "Tell yourself you'll do more than you know you can, and you'll do it, Kata."

Kata couldn't stop thinking of her mother, Edith, three months dead, stone-cold now and alone, with the first autumn leaves falling and winter hurrying behind; the rasp of the wind driving in from the north.

She missed her mother. She wished she'd had more time with her. Kata had never asked enough about her past: how the Swedes had attacked the village and made her a slave on a trading boat. How by some miracle she'd escaped and made it home. Thinking of it made Kata smile. Oh! Think of it! My mother's joy at her escape. Everyone's joy!

Such happiness mixed now with sadness because her mother had gone for ever.

Kata wiped her eyes.

Another memory: standing last summer on top of a stack, helping to thatch it, and Oswald launching himself at her and kissing her cheek, and how she had laughed and pushed him away and he'd fallen right off the stack.

Before she died, Kata's mother had said Kata was turning sixteen, the same as Hilda, and it was high time that she got married. But the boys around here are thickheads, Kata thought. Oswald is the only one either of us could marry, but neither of us wants to, and we can't both have him anyway.

Is this all there is? Kata thought. Ploughing and planting, and weeding, haymaking, harvesting... Round and round and round.

After a while the twins, Odda and Orva, led Wilf the headman's two shire horses down past the cow field to Kata's acre, pulling a cart behind them. Eager and Isen, the two young sons of the reed-cutter Puttnam, were aboard, and so was little Bliss, the three-year-old daughter of Ellette and her husband, the blacksmith Borden, all of them yelping and laughing each time the cart jolted, and urging the twins to go faster, faster...

Eager, who was six, helped Kata and the twins to heave all her barley bundles onto the cart, and once they had, Kata herself climbed on top of them, and threw herself down, exhausted.

Orva scrambled up beside Kata, then Odda whispered secret words into the ears of the horses, and at once they whisked their tails and set off for the great barn.

Orva pulled two grubby lengths of ribbon from inside her shirt. One green, one yellow. "Come on!" she urged. "Sit up, Kata." And she parted Kata's dark brown hair and tied it back with the two ribbons.

"We've rent our clothing," the twins sang out. *"We've rent our clothing, we've tore our skin, to get the headman's harvest in."*

And that was the truth of it. All the healthy men and women of Riccall had helped to bring the harvest home. A small portion of it belonged to each householder, and there was the tithe for the priest, but most of it went to Wilf, the headman, to help him pay tax to the landed lady who owned the village. Wilf was strict, and worked everyone hard, but he was a kind man.

Inside the old barn, several villagers were awaiting the cart. Kata and Orva slid down, and the twins began to fork and toss down the bundles of wheat, then it was the villagers' job to stack them.

Kata, meanwhile, yawned and yawned and kept rubbing her eyes. She slapped the flats of her hands against her body and almost disappeared in a cloud of chaff and dust. Then she went off to find Hilda, wherever she was, to ask her to help make the corncocks.

"Twist them," Kata kept saying to herself, "twist the stalks and shape them – bodies, beaks and tails. Then up the ladder, up and peg them to the gables. Listen, everyone! Listen to them crow. Listen to them sing!"

CHAPTER 3

Before the sun had risen clear of her flaming nightgown, Tor was on his way, leaving Eirik in his grave at the foot of a black cliff and glancing back a couple of times at the shack that had provided him with a second night's shelter.

He hoped he was heading in the right direction, and that his father had not already reached Scarborough.

Probably not, he thought. Before Eirik and Tor had set off from Orkney, Harald had said it would be two days, maybe longer, before he left the harbour there, what with organizing his ships – almost three hundred of them – into small groups and drumming up more support from men loyal to him. Not only that. Harald had brought with him his wife, Queen Ellisif, and Tor's half-sister, Maria, and he wanted to be absolutely sure they would be well looked after while he was busy in England.

Tor picked up a pearly white shell and sent it skimming over the flat, calm water.

And then, thought Tor, on his way to south to Scarborough, my father's meeting Tostig at the mouth of the River Tyne.

Earl Tostig. Well, that's what he was until last year – until the people of York threw him out. Tostig's told my father he's ready to help him attack York, but my father says Tostig has "foxy eyes" and he doesn't trust him.

"But for the moment we're on the same side," King Harald had said. "We both have much to gain from this invasion. For me, the crown of England. For Tostig, the restoration of his earldom of Northumbria."

Despite his hunger, despite his thirst, Tor was in good spirits, and as he strode along the firm dark sand, he whistled or sang snatches of old songs he'd heard from one of the king's poets.

> *"Your sword, Harald. It was so greedy.*
> *While wolves howled from mountain*
> *slopes, you treated ravens to a feast*
> *of corpses. Yes, that year and the next*
> *you ranged east, as far as Jerusalem.*
> *I've never heard of any man*
> *who was a greater warrior."*

Tor whooped, and whooped again, for all that his throat was parched and sore. Thinking of his father's bravery made Tor feel strong. At fifteen – the same age as Tor – his father had proved himself to be a warrior at the Battle of Stiklestad, where Olaf had been killed and, despite being badly wounded, Harald had recovered and sailed to Byzantium to fight for the Empress Zoe.

Tor was proud of his father. And in choosing me as his leading scout, he's shown that he believes in me, thought Tor. "I'm preferring you," Harald had told him. "I'm giving you a great opportunity."

Yes, Tor thought, and now I'm part of my father's saga.

My father has challenged me to help him conquer Britain.

My fate has challenged me.

If I'm bold, thought Tor, bold when it's not easy to be, I should be all right – even without Eirik. He's always been the brave one, the one who took risks, and told me I should too.

For a start, I have to get my story straight. I have to be quite clear about who I am pretending to be so I'm ready when anyone asks me questions.

It's better not to let on that I'm Norwegian, even though lots of Norwegians live in England. I can say I live on the main island of Orkney. What I can't do is tell anyone I'm King Harald's son. No, I'm a fisherman.

My mate Eirik and I were fishing for cod, and we were caught in a skuther, a cat-risper, as we Orcadians say, and driven south… Our boat, *Kittiwake*, she was wrecked and…

And so, as he walked, Tor wove a story about two young fishermen from Orkney who were caught in a windstorm and forced south. How their boat was wrecked and good for nothing but firewood, and how, far worse, his friend Eirik was drowned.

I'll say I want to get home, but don't know how. In that

way, I can talk to traders and boatmen and find out as much about this coast as I can without anyone being suspicious.

All day Tor walked south, and soon after the sun had set, he could see a wide bay ahead of him. Shacks and sheds were scattered below the top of the near shoulder, and under the bay's more precipitous far shoulder huddled a settlement.

Nothing like Trondheim, thought Tor. Not half as big. A hundred dwellings? More, maybe, but the bay looks like a good anchorage. So, is this Scarborough?

In the almost-dark, Tor saw a small group – a family – hurrying towards him.

"Watcha!" a man called out.

"Hi!" replied Tor.

"Where are you going?"

"Here, I think. This is Scarborough, isn't it?"

"Into the arms of the Vikings?"

"What?"

"Haven't you heard? Hardrada … Harald Hardrada's just sailed in. Hundreds of ships!"

"No!" protested Tor. "Where?"

"He's setting up camp somewhere up top. Come the morning, there'll be all hell let loose."

"No!" Tor gasped again.

"Turn yourself around, while you've got time. Head back where you've come from."

Without answering, Tor hurried along the path that followed the shoreline, he passed a small harbour with a few fishing boats anchored in it, and then rounded a headland with what looked like a ruined castle on top of it. Then he saw, opening below him, a second bay – one offering an even more inviting anchorage than the first. And in the gathering gloom, he saw that it was packed with gliding dark shapes. Sliding and slithering through the dark water.

Tor dug his feet into the sand and took a deep breath. *So I didn't get here first. Eirik is dead, and I've got nothing, nothing to report to my father...*

He squeezed his eyelids shut. He had already let his father down. Tor stood rooted to the spot. He didn't want to go a step further, but he knew he had to.

I can't delay, he thought. *I must tell my father what happened to Eirik and to* Kittiwake. *But it's too late to search for his camp tonight; the sun's already setting.*

Tor left the path leading around the bay and walked up a long rise. He worked his way across bristly scrub that scraped his ankles and shins, and then up through a tangled wood, and there he found a deserted shack. It was little different from the one he had left at sunrise except that whoever owned it was using it as his food store.

Fresh fruit, cheese, dried fish, fresh water...

Tor stumbled to his knees. He ate and drank.

"All hell let loose," he said under his breath, and he shivered. "All hell ... in the morning."

That wild cackling. That fierce delight.

Geese. For just a moment Tor thought he was at his mother Solveig's home, lying beside the embers of the fire on her farm in Trondheim Fjord.

Then he jumped up, put his head out of the shack and saw all the wild geese darkening the sky. Thousands and thousands of them, a whole army of pink-footed geese and greylags flying in from Norway and Iceland and Russia on the last leg of their long flight to England and their winter grazing grounds.

As many as our ships, thought Tor, and he began to try to count the birds. No! Far, far more. Thousands, yes, thousands, all of them flying in to help us recapture England.

Recapture England… How can we do that? And on my own, how can I help?

Tor uprooted a pad of damp moss and scrubbed his face with it. Then he sank his teeth into a lump of goat's cheese and squelched several soft plums, devoured a crisp pink apple and swilled it all down with cool, sweet water.

"Now for it!" Tor exclaimed. "My father's camp – up top! That's what that man said. Yes, it's bound to be."

Tor strode up a path leading to the cliff top, and very soon he could see the full extent of the second bay, and the way the Viking fleet was anchored in it, all in groups of nine and ten and twelve, just as the king had disposed them before they all sailed out of Scapa, and left Orkney.

Little service boats, manned by six oarsmen, and carrying provisions and water, were crossing between the larger fighting ships, and now and then Tor could see how the rising sun glanced off the coloured shields lining the gunwales, or picked out their golden pennants.

When he turned around again, and climbed a little further, Tor was able to see Harald's encampment no more than a couple of hundred yards ahead, very close to the top of the cliff, right above the town.

He broke into a run. Past three groups of men, past the

king's skalds, Thjodolf and Arnor, and right up to the king.

"Father!" he shouted. "Father!"

Harald frowned. "Where have you come from?" he demanded. And then, "I thought you'd be here to meet me."

"I know," Tor panted. "So did I."

"Where's Eirik?"

Tor lowered his head. He stared at his feet.

"He was drowned. Our boat capsized."

At once Harald took a step forward and embraced his son in a bear hug.

Tor pulled back and met his father eye to eye. "I'll tell you what happened. And how I buried him, and ask you…"

The king gave him a curt nod. "But not now," he said. "Not now! You can see…" Harald swung round to a group of men who were building a bonfire. "Get a move on," he told them. "Look! There's plenty of firewood down there where Tor's just come from."

King Harald turned back to his son. "Late last evening," he said, "I talked to the headman down there. Him and his elders. They refused this, refused that, refused to surrender the town, and told me they'd talk to me again this morning. Damned Englishmen!"

The king spat on the ground.

"Talk to me this morning!" he barked. "It's me who'll do the talking. Yes, with tongues of flame."

What does he mean? thought Tor. He's not going to burn the place down, is he?

Tor marvelled at his father, and his fury. Look at him! Look! He's the king of the northern world – he's the leader of all these men, all our ships – sometimes so stern, sometimes almost wild. He's my father, but sometimes I scarcely know him.

Harald Hardrada told his men to light the fire, and as soon as the branches were crackling and burning, he seized one himself. He hurled it over the cliff onto the roofs of the wooden buildings right below him.

"Come on!" he shouted. "More! Throw them all over."

Before long, Tor could hear timber crackling and spitting, the roar and updraught of flames blazing, sucking and whistling. He could see men and women and children running away from their huts and shacks; he thought of the old people inside them, unable to escape.

"I've come to help these people," the king shouted to his son. "I've no quarrel with them. No wish to hurt them. But if they resist me… Well, the word will soon spread. This is a warning."

The rising smoke reached the top of the cliff. It wreathed Harald and Tor and dressed them in ashes.

Tor tried to steady his breath and he kept brushing the corners of his eyes.

Harald Hardrada gripped his son's right elbow. "Now then," he growled. "It's time to go down. You, and everyone up here. Go down and take whatever you need."

Tor screwed up his face and stared at the ground.

"For a start, get hold of more clothes and extra footwear. Still wearing sandals! You need boots, boy. Boots!"

Tor nodded. Children running … old people unable to escape…

"And replace whatever you lost when your boat capsized. A net, hooks, tackle. A sharp knife and whetstone."

Tor sniffed.

"Get hold of a sack. Stuff it with food. Bread, dried fish, horsemeat. Take whatever you want. It's all ours."

The king slapped his son's back. "I know you. I've seen how you've always got an eye for a pretty girl. Keep right away from them."

Tor shook his head. He couldn't stop thinking about all the flames, the children, his father's cruelty... He hadn't got the least intention of going down into the burning town, and reckoned he could quickly pick up provisions and boots and everything on his way south.

"You understand? You take what you need."

"Yes, sire."

"Listen," said Harald. "Your capsizing, and Eirik drowning. This is your chance to prove yourself."

"On my own," said Tor, and he knew he sounded more nervous than he meant to.

"Why ever not? I was wounded, very badly wounded, when I was fifteen. The same age as you."

"I know," said Tor in a low voice. "My mother, she helped to carry you from the battlefield."

"She did. She smuggled me away to her family's farm. And but for her, I wouldn't be standing here now."

"And but for you, Father..." Tor began.

Harald laughed and slapped Tor on the back. "You wouldn't either! This is your chance, Tor! As you know, we're heading for York, but I've heard from traders that the Ouse – the river that runs up to York – narrows before it reaches the city. In some places it's no more than thirty paces across. And there are shallows... So I can't sail my fleet right up to

York. We'll have to anchor south of the city. Now then! I'm going to sail south as far as the Humber. I've already posted scouts down the coast. What I want you to do is scout the land west of that – up the Humber and the Derwent, then up the Ouse."

Tor nodded.

"On either side," the king went on, "there are outlying farms, the watermills, the villages. Check them out. How many householders there are in each of them. See what we'll be facing and where it's best for us to anchor."

"Yes, sire."

"The first thing to decide is how you're going to get there. It's a long trek south. You'll need a horse or a strong pony." Harald drummed his fingers on his chest. "Steal one, or even better, find a trader ship to take you. Use your silver tongue to get yourself on board."

Tor almost smiled, and he nodded.

"I'm relying on you, Tor. Find me a place to anchor on the Ouse. Three hundred ships! We'll meet somewhere south of York, and you'll have plenty to tell me."

"Yes, sire. I will."

"All right! I'll see you at the gates of York. Skedaddle!"

CHAPTER 4

Most of the people living in Riccall had heard the church bell and were already gathered in the lofty barn. They were gossiping and joking and admiring the way in which the women had not only set out the harvest feast but decorated the ledges and stacks with apples, pears and plums and wooden platters of hazelnuts, bunches of onions and shallots and parsnips, as well as jars brimming with sloes and blackberries.

When the priest advanced to the centre of the barn with the headman, and Wilf clapped his hands, almost everyone hushed.

You can tell at once that he's a leader, thought Kata. I've heard my mother's first man was like that when he was our headman. Firm and calm.

"Now!" Wilf began. "I've got news." Wilf looked round. Everyone in the barn was staring him straight in the eye.

"Snell and Rinan sailed in an hour ago. This was their big summer trawl down the three rivers – right out to the coast. When they beached at Holderness, they talked to fishermen from the north, further than Scarborough. Yes... That's when they heard that the King of Norway, Harald Hardrada, is sailing south down the coast with a huge fleet."

Cries and shouts echoed round and round the barn.

The headman nodded and pursed his mouth. "They're likely making for York. After all, whoever controls York controls the whole of the north of England. And as you know there's only one way there. Into the Humber, then up the Ouse..."

Our Ouse, thought Kata, and then up here to Riccall.

"Praise be to God we got the harvest home," Hilda's mother, Mattie, called out.

Wilf pushed out his lower lip. "I suppose so," he said. "Unless the Vikings stay and help themselves."

Or torch the barn, thought Kata, and she shivered. Riccall was a natural stopping point for them, because then the river narrowed all the way up to York.

"What's worse," said Wilf, "is that the same fishermen from up north told Snell and Rinan that Earl Tostig is joining forces with King Harald."

"The coward!" shouted Puttnam, the reed-cutter.

"Worse than that," yelled Mattie, always quick to praise and quick to condemn. "He's a traitor!"

"Yes, a traitor!"

By now, many of the villagers were raising their voices.

"Why isn't he here?"

"Shoulder to shoulder with us!"

"He wants to be king, King of all England."

"He'll stop at nothing."

Wilf waited for them to peter out before speaking again.

"Very likely the Vikings will put in for provisions somewhere. We should be prepared for the worst – the Viking fleet sailing straight up here – but my bet is they'll call in on Scarborough first. There are two bays there. Big ones. Safe anchorage. And the town is right next to them. If I were headman up there, I'd be having bad dreams."

Kata shivered again. Why do warnings and fear make us feel cold? she wondered. It's a warm morning, and yet I'm freezing.

"It took Snell and Rinan three days to come up from the coast, because they met headwinds," Wilf said, "but they've eased now. That's good for the Vikings, bad for us. So this is what I reckon. We'll send a small boat downriver in the morning so we can check where the Vikings are and get as much warning as we can. We need three of you to be our scouts."

"Me!" Hilda called out.

At once Mattie rounded on her. "That you won't!" she told her daughter.

Hilda rolled her eyes at Kata, and Kata smiled, but at once she felt sad her own mother wasn't there.

"Me!" declared Oswald.

Wilf shook his head. "No, I'll need your help here. You too, Hilda. Snell and Rinan, you're our watermen! I think you should be our scouts, and maybe Odda should go with you."

"Now!" said the headman. There's plenty to do here.

For a start, we must round up all our animals, and be ready to drive them away from Riccall."

There was a horrified silence, and then cries of dismay.

"Away?"

"Where?"

"Have you ever rounded up a coop of chickens?"

"Or argued with goats?"

Wilf waited calmly. "Listen!" he said. "Ships are sailed by men, and men need feeding. If the Vikings see our livestock, they'll likely lay-up and slaughter them even if they don't slaughter us."

"You know my goats, Wilf," a voice called out from the back of the barn.

"Well, if they'd prefer to be supper for hungry Vikings," Wilf replied, "that's up to them! Listen! If there's no one around, no people and no animals, Harald may sail on upriver. He won't want his men to stray too far from their ships in search of food. We must get out of the village. If we can put a few miles between us, and hide our livestock, then I reckon we should be safe."

After this, almost everyone began to talk and argue.

"I've prayed this would never happen again," groaned Mattie. "Each day, I have."

"Nineteen years," said Snell. "It's nineteen since the Swedes attacked us."

"God moves in mysterious ways," Father Huw called out. "He does what's right for His children."

Kata's heart pounded. The Swedish raiders took my mother, Edith, for a slave, she thought, and her life must have been so tough, working from dawn to dusk, and being slapped and even thrashed. She found just one friend – a Norwegian girl, travelling south somewhere to meet her father – and they talked and shared memories and sometimes teamed up against the merchants. My mother said they were like sisters and without her my mother wouldn't have survived.

Is the same thing happening all over again? First the Swedes, now the Vikings. And if it is, will they take me to be a slave? Or Hilda? Or both of us? From the things I've heard about them, their cruelty, I'd rather die.

"Well, there's one thing," said Puttnam. "I've never known so much rain this time of year. The reed beds are brimming. If the Vikings lay-up here, plenty will drown in the swamp, just stepping from boat to boat, and boat to breastwork, and that."

That's true, thought Kata. The rain almost wrecked our harvest. Old Kendra thinks it's because of the comet, and it'll go on raining until the comet disappears. So maybe we'll be safe.

The talk in the barn was like a tide. First it had been about what to do if the Vikings did sail up to Riccall, but then it turned to the Vikings themselves and especially their leader, Harald Hardrada.

"Me and Ellette met these Norwegians up in York," Borden said, "we were up in Coppergate to buy her a necklace when we got married. They told us King Harald's a whole head taller than, well – than you, Wilf, and you, Puttnam, and any usual man."

"And his fists," added Ellette, "they're like clubs."

"Crafty, that's what he is," said old Kendra, "crafty and

cruel. He always has been. Haven't you heard what he did when he laid siege to a town away down south? He netted dozens of house martins, same as nest here, and his men tied lighted twigs to their tail feathers, and when the martins flew back to their nests, they set fire to the town."

"No!" cried Hilda, and she buried her head in her hands.

"Horrible!" cried Kata.

"That's not half of it," Kendra went on. "With his own hands he strangled an emperor. The Emperor of Zantium, wherever that is."

"When Harald was wounded," Puttnam told Oswald, "he was the same age as you. Only fifteen. He went right on fighting. A spear in his stomach only made him stronger. Even fiercer than before."

"I'm sixteen," said Oswald. "Rising seventeen." He grinned at Kata, but Kata compressed her lips and refused to look at him.

Some of the things the villagers told each other were true, but some – Kata suspected – were not, but just hearsay, the gossip of Norwegian merchants sailing up and down the Ouse.

Suddenly a rat scuttled out from between two bales and bolted for the door.

Oswald grabbed a pitchfork, but he wasn't quick enough.

"Drat!" he exclaimed. And still holding his weapon, he whirled round, and by mistake stabbed Mattie's backside.

Kata gasped.

Mattie screeched and grabbed herself, and her daughter, Hilda, inspected the wound. "Nothing much," she declared. "Just bloodied!"

"Nothing much!" shouted Mattie, and she staggered back against a pile of wheat bundles. The whole stack rocked and fell sideways, knocking over her daughter, and half burying them both.

Puttnam's boys, Eager and Isen, yelled in delight and at once piled in on top of them. Many of the villagers laughed, and then Kata reached out with both hands and pulled Hilda and her mother to their feet.

When they had dusted themselves down, Old Kendra announced, "What that means, Hilda, is you'll get married. Yes, you'll marry within the year."

"Who says?" retorted Hilda. "You just made that up."

"Those as know things don't need to make them up," Kendra replied. She stared at Hilda and narrowed her eyes.

"Not to anyone here, I'm not," Hilda retorted, and she exchanged a look with Kata.

Wilf clapped his hands.

"All right now! That's enough of that. We're all in this together, and you must all sort yourselves out – and your animals. I must ride up to York."

"York!" exclaimed several voices. "Why?"

"Why do you think?" said Wilf. "I must tell the earls. Morcar. Edwin. I must warn them as soon as I can."

"What will they do?" Oswald asked. "The earls?"

"They'll send messengers at once to King Harold Godwinson, and ask for help, but he's hundreds of miles away on the south coast watching out for Duke William and the Normans. The question is, how long can the earls hold out against the Vikings?"

Then Odda asked what Kata knew was bound to be troubling the men, old and young, "What about us? Will we have to fight?"

Wilf gave a faint smile. "Without weapons?" he replied. "You can't fight without weapons."

"Oswald's got a pitchfork!" Mattie called out, still clutching her backside, and several people snorted.

Yes, and he's good at killing mice, Kata thought.

"Scythes, sickles, sticks, crooks, short knives, you can't fight with those," said Wilf. "Not for long. Our law says that if the king raises an army, he can require one man from each family to join him. No! Our duty is to make things difficult for the Vikings here and delay them for as long as we can, not to fight them."

It's strange in here, thought Kata, and I can't properly describe it. It's such a mixture. Being afraid but also laughing … being more together… Just when I thought nothing would change, and everything would stay the same for ever. The Vikings! Harald! And rounding up our animals and leaving the village. Kata's thoughts were swirling round and round inside her head.

"It's too late to ride up to York and back again before dark," Wilf told them. "So I'll go early tomorrow. Well, Kata, are you coming with me?"

"Me?"

Wilf nodded.

"Why me?"

"I'm thinking I could do with a bit of company," Wilf replied.

It's because of my mother, thought Kata. Wilf's being

kind because she's died and he's honouring me because her first husband was headman.

"Kata?"

"Yes," she said eagerly. "Yes, I'm coming."

"Now," said Wilf, turning back to the villagers. "Father Huw and I have spoken, and we both agree that we should all enjoy the fruits of this year's harvest. Enjoy them as best we can. I know that in some years past you've still been drinking at dawn, and you won't want to be doing that. But eat, drink, and listen to Father Huw's wise words."

So that's what the people of Riccall did.

Father Huw's little sermon was the same each year, just as much as the trestle tables charged with food and the horns and jugs of ale and mead. His words were part of what linked one harvest home to the previous one and to the next. They were a sort of charm. They were what joined the people of Riccall to people they had never met in villages the length and breadth of Holy England.

The priest nodded fondly at his flock. "Hunger is the worst of enemies," he said. "The worst! It makes the strong weak. It makes the hopeful hopeless. But once again, by the grace of God, we've been granted a fine harvest. Bread is the staff of life!"

CHAPTER 5

Light footsteps, pattering...

Kata sat up, and the door swung open. Three moon faces and three little bodies blocked out the early light.

"Cor!"

"It's dark in there."

Giggling and shoving...

"Are you wearing any clothes?"

"Of course I am!" Kata replied. "Why? Aren't you?"

More giggling...

"What do you want?" Kata demanded.

"Up at the barn they want you," said Eager.

"Why?"

"Mattie says it's your turn for ratting. You and Hilda." He took a step into the hut.

"Get out!" Kata laughed.

"What's this? Can you eat it?" Eager reached out for

something lying on the ground beside Kata's pallet.

"You heard me. Get out."

Eager held his ground. "Wilf says the rats were busy all night."

"They even ate the sloes," said Isen, his younger brother.

"And the woefuls," little Bliss added.

"The what?" asked Kata.

Eager reached out for the rusk or whatever it was on the ground.

"Get out, I said!" Kata ordered him. "All three of you. You little rats!"

As soon as the children had gone, Kata jumped up and dashed water over her face from the bucket outside the door.

Early tomorrow, she thought. That's what Wilf said yesterday. I can't do the ratting as well as go up to York.

So she hurried over to the headman's croft, and tapped on the door with her left forefinger.

She tapped again.

Then Kata let herself in and saw at once that the headman was still lying on his pallet.

"Oh, Wilf!" she exclaimed. "Not today."

"The one thing I have in common with King Alfred," he groaned.

"What?"

"Our bellies." The headman belched. "But he ruled Wessex and fought the Vikings. I can't even ride as far as York."

Kata knelt beside him.

"It's like something is twisting and crawling inside me, and none of Kendra's cures are the least help." The headman tucked his knees under his chin.

Kata nodded. "I know. You've tried them all."

"I have. And all Kendra does is grunt, and shake her head, and say 'Filthied! Filthied stomach!'"

The effort to speak was making the headman's face shiny with sweat.

"I should be up tomorrow. I must talk to the earls as soon as I can."

So that was that. Or it would have been, but Wilf called after her, "Kata! Kata!"

"What?"

"The little boat."

"What boat?"

"With three scouts."

"I know," Kata said. "To check where the Vikings are."

"Snell and Rinan and Odda," the headman whispered. And then he closed his eyes.

After she had left Wilf's croft, Kata paused and shook her head. Only last evening, she thought, I believed everything was changing, changing at last, but now it's changing again, what with me not going to York, not yet anyhow. But things feel strange – they feel different. Like this is a waiting time. Like when you see dark clouds riding in, and swelling, and you know that before long there'll be a storm.

CHAPTER 6

To Tor's left were broad flat sands and the glittering German Ocean. To his right, distant, purplish moorland. And ahead? Ahead lay sweeping green England, so empty, so wide open, and waiting for him.

Hurrying south, always within sight of the ocean, he stopped off from time to time at stony, isolated farms where he told his sad story about sailing south from Orkney and about the boat wreck and his poor dead friend, and he charmed women and their daughters with his courteous manners and asked them questions about their lives and livestock, before swiping some item while their backs were turned, and making off as soon as he could. Here, a well-made small cutting knife, its grip bound with a twisted strip of leather, just right for chopping up pieces of meat. There, a worn grindstone for sharpening his knife. There, a pair of baggy trousers and a length of frayed rope. And a piece of scraped calfskin that Tor quickly rolled up and stuffed inside his shirt.

On the third evening, lying in a sand dune, well sheltered from the wind, and well fed with a cooked partridge he had stolen from the last farm kitchen he had visited, Tor listened to the whispering-and-shuffling sea.

Me and Eirik and *Kittiwake*, he thought, we should be skimming down here. Past all these cliffs and old earthworks and gritty beaches and caves. It's going to take me too long to get up the Ouse and near to York if I have to walk all the way. I must get a pony, like my father said.

Early next morning, hungry again and thirsty, Tor followed the track round the back of a cliff, and he passed a couple of tumbledown buildings better suited to animals than humans before he came to a farm fronted by a paddock with three ponies grazing in it.

Tor filled his lungs. Slowly he exhaled. And again. Then he ran across the paddock to the nearest pony, vaulted onto his back and dug his heels into his flanks.

The pony dug in his heels too.

"Come on!" Tor urged it. "*Olé!* Come on! *Olé!*"

Then the pony sprang forward, and Tor was all but thrown over his tail. The pony grunted, snorted and sprang forward again, and this time he didn't stop.

The farmer and his family were all down at the bottom of the west field, harvesting, and the last thing in the world they expected was some stranger appearing over the cliffs, and making off with one of their precious ponies.

Their two hounds heard the pony's snorting, though. And when they heard Tor shouting, they raced up to the paddock. Furiously barking, they chased Tor, and one of them kept snapping at his right foot. Then it leapt up and bit his calf.

Tor kicked at the dog and he stabbed it in one shoulder with his cutting knife, and the dog yelped, and fell back. So did his companion. Mournfully they howled, and Tor was in the clear.

After this, the pony became quite obliging, and responded well to Tor's easy, expert touch, his commands and cajoling. And for his part, Tor was pleased to have company.

For a full hour he rode south, along the wide track he had followed all the way from Scarborough, before he came to a windswept beach, and at the far end of it, a stunted ash tree. Certain at last that no one could catch him up, Tor dismounted, made a noose from the frayed rope he had pilfered, and tied the pony to the tree.

"Now let's have a look at you," he said, and he walked around the pony several times ... appraising him. Strong shoulders ... hindquarters...

"Very strong, you are. Yes, fine hocks."

The pony listened and gave Tor quite a kindly look.

"You're calm, too. Well, once you'd calmed down. And ... here! I like the silky feathering on your legs."

The pony snuffled.

"Not as strong as my own pony, though," said Tor. "His heavy shoulders. His silver tail. My brave Leif."

For a moment Tor was standing not on the east coast of England but back home in the field above the fjord where he had grown up, like his mother, and many generations before them. He was cutting Leif's coarse mane so that it stood right up, with the black strip in the middle a little higher than the white strips on either side of it.

Think! Just think if we all had our own hair cut like that. We could lighten the outer strips with chalk or darken the centre strip with … I don't know what, and it would make us look much taller than we really are.

Not that my father needs anything like that. No, he's a head taller than anyone else already.

Tor took the pony's head between his hands and rubbed his own forehead against it.

"Come on!" he said. "We're both hungry and both thirsty, and I'm sore from riding you without a saddle. I must get a saddle somewhere."

On they went, and before long Tor was able to filch some hay to feed the pony and find a dew pond where they could quench their thirst.

"So what's your name?" he asked the pony. "And what am I going to call you? I don't know… How about Skopti? It's a good, strong Norse name."

That night, Tor rested out of the wind – and neither the shrieking of the birds nor Skopti's snoring disturbed him.

On again, on and on until at last they reached the estuary of a wide river.

It's as wide as the mouth of Trondheim Fjord, thought Tor. Even wider. Is this the River Humber? It must be, yes!

Tor trotted along a narrow strip of rising ground that stood proud of the salt water swilling almost all around it. He shaded his eyes and saw how the track now swung away to the west, along the banks of the estuary, towards the setting sun.

Only then did he see that there was a staithe almost beneath him – a little haven, with a large boat tied up to the landing stage.

Then Tor saw the runes cut deep into the boat's prow.

Mævill.

Seagull!

Norwegian, thought Tor. But the sail and the rigging, they don't look Norwegian ... and neither do the oars...

If they're going upstream, I can talk myself aboard. Me and Skopti. That's exactly what my father suggested. And I'll be able to scout for several days before he catches up with me.

Tor rode straight down to the haven.

"Hi!" he called out. "Hi!"

The great tongue of the boat's square sail drew in a breath of wind and billowed.

"Hi!" Tor called again, and then two dark-skinned men appeared from behind it.

"Hi!" one of them answered. It wasn't a greeting, more a kind of assessment. A sort of question.

Tor swung himself off his pony, bounded along the landing plank and clapped hands with one of the men. And at once he started to fire questions in English at them.

"Where are you going? York? Where have you come from?"

One man held up his hands. "Wait!" he said. "Skipper!"

Tor grinned. "Can't you even speak English?" he asked.

The man clattered down a short ladder and before long

reappeared, followed by a small, stocky, red-headed man and a dark-skinned woman.

At once Tor stepped towards the man and held out his right hand.

The skipper narrowed his eyes. "Go on then. Who are you?"

Tor took a deep breath. He carefully explained how he and Eirik had been blown off course from Orkney, right across Pentland Firth and down the east coast, and how they were wrecked north of Scarborough, and Eirik had been drowned. "I'm heading for York," he said. "I've heard it's my best chance of picking up passage back to Orkney."

"And King Harald?" the skipper asked. "What have you heard about him?"

Tor shrugged and stuck out his lower lip. He didn't answer.

"Really? Surely everyone up in Orkney has heard about his plans. You're one of the settlers there?"

Tor nodded. "That's right. I'm not a Viking. Certainly not!"

"I'll tell you what I've been hearing all summer. How Hardrada's planning one more expedition. One last mission. To claim the kingdom of England. If that's so, the first place he'll make for is bound to be York. Same as us. And if Earl Morcar – the young earl – if he tries to resist, there'll be a bloodbath." The skipper drew his right forefinger across his throat. "You. Me. All of us." Then he pointed at himself. "Matason," he said.

"Strange name," said Tor. "It's not Norwegian."

"Half Ireland, half Iceland. And her, she's Safæ. My ship-wife."

Safæ politely inclined her head.

Tor smiled. "I'm Tor," he said. "And your boat? It's not Norwegian either, is it?"

Matason shook his head. "Irish," he said. "She was built by Norsemen in Dublin. *Mævill*, yes. Seagull!" He fingered his red beard. "All right, Tor. I'll give you passage."

"You will?" Tor said eagerly.

"If you work your way."

"Of course."

"And give me the pony."

There was an awkward silence.

"Well, he's…"

"Not yours to give," Matason said, slowly.

Tor screwed up his face.

"I thought not," said the skipper.

"I was hoping to trade him for passage back to Orkney," lied Tor.

"Your choice," said Matason.

So Tor sort of hummed, and hesitated. But he'd already decided to take Matason's offer.

This boat will get me close to York much more quickly than Skopti, he thought. And during the night, I'll jump ship and start to scout the river, how wide it is, the settlements along it, and everything.

So he shook hands with the skipper without meaning to keep his part of the bargain.

"I'll tell you, though," Matason said, eyeing him carefully, as though he half-suspected him. "We trade trust and understanding. We trade peace."

"What do you mean?" Tor asked.

"I mean," said the skipper, almost thrusting the point of his beard into Tor's face, "we know the merchants in York, and they know us. We argue, we bargain, but for many years now, there's been no fighting." He pursed his mouth and gave Tor a knowing look. "Vikings mean trouble. But … enough of this. You hungry?"

"What?"

"You deaf?"

"No, no!" exclaimed Tor. "I'm famished. I could eat a horse!"

The skipper threw back his head, laughed and pointed at Tor's pony. "Bring the pony over," Matason said. "Bring him over. He can tell us his story."

And that's what happened. The two slaves hoisted a kind of floppy canopy in the stern, Matason's ship-wife, Safæ, went below deck to prepare food. And the skipper, meanwhile, rolled a barrel of ale from the bows to the stern.

As the sun set, the calm, wide water of the estuary first shone blood-orange, and then faded and turned pink. Stars started to appear, and Tor easily picked out the Giant's Belt and then the Plough, as he had so often done at his mother's farm, and in Orkney.

For a while the little group sat listening to the pony munching mouthfuls of hay, the slap and slop of the water against the boat, the night air breathing in the canopy. Matason told Tor they had docked only that afternoon, after an easy passage from Ribe, and said they were carrying skins and furs, and a fine supply of eiderdown, and a ton of whetstones.

"And that's where I sold my last two slaves – worse than

useless – and bought these two. Razon and Mundir. They came from Africa."

Then the skipper placed three hunks of tallow on the capstan in the stern, and lit them from the ever-light, and the five of them sat inside their glowing tent. For an hour and maybe longer they left time outside it, and Tor was relieved not to have to think for a while about his duties as a scout or about his father and the Viking fleet.

Matason leant into the candlelight, and his shadow on the canopy loomed over them. Tor lifted his mug of ale. Theft and trickery and honour, they all lay muddied at the bottom of it.

CHAPTER 7

Through a curtain of dawn drizzle, Tor saw that *Mavill* was surrounded by shining slakes and floating only on a very narrow creek leading to the broad reach of the river.

Sailing here must be much more difficult than in the fjord, he thought. All this silt! And that long bank of shingle.

For a while he watched dozens of gulls squabbling and then dispersing as three storks splashed down, white as fresh snow.

That's good luck. Three… Or is it seven? Seven birds? Both, I think.

Tor heard someone coming up the short ladder. Matason it was, and for a while they stood side by side staring out across the estuary.

"Rain, and then even more rain," said the skipper. "Too much rain falls on England."

"Same as Orkney," said Tor.

"The sandbanks and shingle shift each year," Matason told him. "The creeks widen, they close up. I've known this river half my life, yet each spring I think I scarcely know it at all."

"When will we get to York then?"

"Depends. The tide ... the wind... Sometime tomorrow. Or the next day. Maybe I'll lay-up at Blacktoft."

"Where?"

"Blacktoft. Where this river and the Trent and Ouse all meet."

"Ouse," Tor repeated. This was working out exactly as he'd hoped.

"Good name, no?" said Matason. "Though when sheets of rain fall up on the moors, the water doesn't ooze – it rushes down the river and floods all those water meadows between Fulford and Riccall."

So there and then Tor decided to jump ship at Blacktoft and walk the last part of the journey to York.

I'll be able to scout the route all the more carefully on foot, he thought. And find out how far the fleet will be able to sail up the Ouse. How far short of York they'll be. Where they can best anchor and disembark.

My father's got three hundred ships! Nine thousand men!

And then I'll try to retrieve my pony from Matason in York. Skopti and me, we've only been companions for a short time, but he has such a friendly expression. I don't want to leave him behind.

As soon as they moored at Blacktoft, Tor swept up his sea coat and small belongings and, clutching his stomach, ran off towards a willow tree, shouting, "I'll be back! I've been caught short! I'll be back!"

When he was beyond the willow, and hidden by it, Tor hared away inland. He hurried west and then north across open, flat country without a single tree or hedgerow, and only rejoined the course of the river two miles or so upstream. Then twice the river looped – it almost looped around him – and Tor was able to take short cuts across more unused land.

It's not like home, he thought. Not at all. Norway is so bony. Where it's workable at all, we have to use each and every acre.

Still early in the afternoon, Tor came upon a stone slab standing upright on a small mound on the riverbank, and when he looked closely, he saw runes cut into it.

"Bergvid," Tor read. "Bergvid raised this stone... His son..." Tor tried to decipher the missing words, but time and rough weather had worn them away. The son's name and the runes following it were gone.

"... drowned here," Tor spelled out. "He was a good lad."

Tor got onto his knees and clutched the slab. He thought of Eirik; he thought of the two fishermen whose skiff had collided with a submerged wedge of ice in Trondheim Fjord only the year before; he thought of all his own blood relatives, and their salty gravestones around the jetty below his mother's farm.

He wouldn't have been able to explain why, but all at once he stood up, swiftly stripped himself naked, and plunged into the dark pool eddying beside the riverbank.

The surface water was tepid, the lower level, so cool. The depths almost cold.

It's like time passing, he thought. It is, almost. Today ... and yesterday ... all the cold days and years before.

Tor rose, gasping. He swept back his long, fair hair, and then he grabbed a handful of rushes by the roots and rubbed himself all over with them.

Then he rose from the pool, roused and quick, innocent of the salt waves of the ocean, the ashes of Scarborough, the dust of the dirt track down to the Humber, untroubled by his small sins.

Me, he thought, I'm alive. Alive! And I'll live each and every hour to the utmost!

Tor heard it from a long way off. Slamming and grinding, roaring and rushing. Quick and slow, he approached it – a watermill standing on the riverbank.

True, *Mævill* had sailed past two mills early that morning, on the way to Blacktoft, but he had never seen one close-up, and for a while he stood and marvelled at it.

The way part of the water flowing downstream had been dammed and diverted to make a mill race and drive the machinery. The huge wheel, cut from oak, slowly turning, and the shaft and gear wheel banded in iron...

Tor shuffled up to the entrance, and stepped in. It was gloomy, and the air was thicker than outside, and chaff was flying all over the place. Deafening too, with the mill race thrashing below him.

But while he was still standing there, Tor was grabbed by the back of his sea coat, thrown off balance, and dragged right out of the mill.

"Hey!" he protested.

But whoever it was turned Tor over and drove him down onto his knees.

"I've had enough of you ruffians, messing around in here."

Tor looked up. A big man. Burly. With a spade of a grey beard.

And the man looked down and scowled. "Who are you, anyhow?" he demanded. "With your fair hair ... blue eyes. Not one of those Vikings?"

"No!" Tor scrambled to his feet. With the flats of his hands, he swiped the chaff off his smock and trousers.

"Where are you from?"

"Orkney," said Tor, with a half-smile.

"Never heard of it. What you doing here?"

"Where am I?"

The man frowned. "Riccall!" he said loudly.

"Riccall!" exclaimed Tor.

"Where have you been all your life? Me, I'm the miller. Name's Bullfrog."

Tor pointed downriver. "I was on a trader, sailing over from Ribe. At noon the captain put in at Blacktoft."

"Go on then. What's brought you here?"

"I got caught short!" Tor smiled. "And when I came back, the boat had gone. They left without me."

The miller stared at Tor and chafed his pink lips. "Rubbish!" he exclaimed. "I don't believe a word of it."

Tor shrugged.

"No boat's been through here in the last two days. What are you up to?"

"Walking! Walking to York."

"Walking to York, are you," scoffed the miller. "And why is that?"

"Why do you think?" Tor asked indignantly. "To catch up with my boat."

"I've told you," the miller said. "No boat's been through here in the last two days. I should know. I have to lead each one by the nose to get through this gut. Each one! Me and my two horses."

Tor and the miller heard a shout and saw three people lurching towards them along the path between the marshy riverbank and a field of cabbages. Each of them was carrying a sack over one shoulder, heavy as a corpse.

"Ah!" Bullfrog exclaimed. "Oswald. And Kata and Hilda."

Tor shrugged.

"We've got a visitor," the miller called out. "Seen him before?"

The three of them stared at Tor, and Tor stared at them. Much the same age as me, he thought. All three of them. One of the girls was very pretty.

"Skulking around. Says he got left behind by a trader, so he's walking up to York to rejoin it. Drivel! I don't even know his name," growled Bullfrog.

"You haven't asked me," Tor replied, and he swept back his fair hair.

"Well, what is it?" asked the pretty girl. "I'm Kata. And this is Hilda, and Oswald."

"Tor. I'm Tor."

At this moment, Tor caught Kata's eye, and she caught his, and he winked at her.

Bullfrog screwed up his face. "Tor? Boar, jaw, war... What kind of name is that?"

"It's Norse," Tor explained politely. "Some people say Thor."

"Thor," said Oswald, "He's the thunder god." He looked at Kata, but she was looking at Tor. "You a Viking then?"

Tor shook his head. "Certainly not," he said. "I come from Orkney."

Bullfrog cleared his throat and spat on the ground.

Oswald jerked up his head.

"From what I've heard," said Tor, "there are more Norwegians than Saxons over here. Is that right?"

"Too damned many," replied the miller. "And thousands more on their way. That's what Snell and Rinan told me."

"I don't know about that," said Tor. He turned to Kata. "You live here?"

Oswald put an arm around Kata. "We all do," he said.

When Tor glanced at Kata again, she was already looking at him, and they both smiled. Then Kata lowered her head.

This time Hilda noticed. Oswald too. His mouth tightened, and he gave Tor a stony look.

Bullfrog scrubbed his grey beard. Tor could tell he was suspicious and maybe even wondering whether Tor had anything to do with the Viking fleet...

The miller smiled a grim smile. "Well, you clear off. There's nothing for you here – no one and nothing – and I got to grind this barley. You three clear off too," he said to Kata, Hilda and Oswald. "Kata, you're heading to York tomorrow, aren't you? To warn the earls about the Vikings."

Tor straightened his back. Kata was going to York.

"Maybe I'll see you there," he said.

CHAPTER 8

The next morning Wilf was waiting for Kata outside his open door.

"Did you hear him?" he asked.

"Who?"

"Our screech owl. Round and round the village all night."

Kata shook her head. "I was with the angels," she said.

"A pretty saying," Wilf replied. "But I doubt angels need much sleep. Anyhow, all that ghastly screaming would have woken them up."

Kata yawned. That night, she had been restless. First, she felt flushed, then she felt cold, this on a warm September night. And once, her heart began to thresh. That boy. Tor. Might she really see him in York? He had winked at her yesterday. She was sure he did. His eyes were bright blue. And fast as a shooting star, she thought. So fast that Oswald and Hilda, standing beside her, didn't notice it.

The headman and Kata collected their saddles and tackle from the barn and walked round to the paddock.

"You're feeling better," Kata said.

"As you can see," Wilf replied. "*Deo gratias!*"

Not long after they rode out of Riccall, the wind picked up from the west and gave the elm trees and weeping willows a good shaking.

The elderberries and blackberries trembled in the hedgerows, and crowds of goldfinches hurled themselves to and fro gathering seeds, as if there were not a moment to be lost.

What with water hurrying down the river, thought Kata, and Snell and Rinan and Odda nosing downstream ... and the Viking fleet, creeping down the coast... Everything's on the move. My heart, I know my heart's on the move too, but I can't exactly explain it.

Tor! Is it true what you said about not being a Viking? I don't care whether you're telling the gospel truth or a pack of lies. I don't care at all.

Once they had passed Green Hill, Kata and the headman left the riverbank to avoid the marshes and took the old track leading to Kelfield. By the time they rejoined the river path, it was raining hard.

"The kind of rain that doesn't mean to stop," Wilf said in disgust. "Not until nightfall."

The two of them pulled up for the first time when they came to a place where the rivers Ouse and Wharfe met, and the water was kicking up and almost boiling.

Wilf waved at the Wharfe. "Know what's up there?"

Kata shook her head and water trickled down the back

of her neck. "I never even saw them, but Oswald told me our ships are up there…"

Oswald, she thought. He didn't like Tor at all. And the way he put his arm around me, like I was his. Kata shivered. I'm not Oswald's.

"Eyes like a hawk, that Oswald," said the headman. "Nineteen of our ships, yes. They've tucked themselves right up here, out of harm's way."

"But what if the Vikings—"

"No! They'd only be able to get past the watermill one by one. And Bullfrog would know about it. They wouldn't risk it. Too exposed. There are lots of shallows up there, too, and narrows where you can't even sail two abreast."

As they rode on, Kata started to tell the headman how she and Oswald and Hilda had met a boy from Orkney at the watermill on the previous afternoon. "He was nosing around."

"He was, was he?"

"Yes, and walking right up to York!"

Wilf listened. He pursed his lips. "Oh! So that's it, is it?"

"What do you mean?"

At first the headman didn't reply. "Norwegians behind us, Norwegians ahead of us … and now your boy."

"Tor," said Kata. She liked being able to say his name out loud.

"Well, it's a good thing he didn't wake you," Wilf told her.

"Who?"

"The screech owl."

"Why? What do you mean?"

Wilf slowly turned to Kata in his saddle. "A warning

of danger and death, isn't it, a screech owl," he said. "Ask Kendra."

A warning, thought Kata. What kind of danger? Tor's not dangerous.

Now the river eased into long loops, and Wilf named the farms and features on either side of it.

"Heverland Farm and Halfpenny Hill and over there Naburn Ings, Fulford Ings..."

"What does that mean?" Kata asked. "Ings? I've heard it ever so often."

"Marshes," said Wilf. "Water meadows. Fields that get flooded when the river's in spate."

"Look, Wilf! Look! All those houses."

True, there were more and more timber warehouses lining the opposite riverbank.

"So many," said Kata, shaking her head.

As the Ouse wound into York, Kata kept exclaiming and pointing out until at last they reached the high stone walls, and the massive gate through them.

"They enclose the whole city," Wilf told her. "Built by Romans a thousand years ago."

The great stone walls, yes, and a bridge crossing the river, two stone churches, and the huge castle on its mound.

"Is that it?" marvelled Kata. "Where the earls live?"

"No, that's even further."

Kata drew up, let go of her reins, and embraced the city.

"The largest city in the whole of the north of England," Wilf told her. "And the most rich."

"No wonder Hardrada wants to attack it."

"Some years ago," said Wilf, "our kingdom was ruled

by the Norwegians. That's why Harald thinks York is his by right."

"It's not, is it?"

"Over the years," Wilf said, "I've often heard the same story: Norwegian merchants saying that Harald Hardrada has no quarrel with us, and just wants to reclaim York and our kingdom."

"So why is he coming with hundreds of warships?" Kata asked.

"That's the right question," Wilf said, as he and Kata rode into the courtyard in front of the residence of the Earls of Northumbria. "He wouldn't be attacking us – but for Earl Tostig. Tostig! Our king's own brother. His greed, his lust for power. From what I've heard, he's spent the whole summer egging Harald on to invade us, and now scouts have reported that he's sailing up from somewhere south to join forces with him."

Wilf and Kata were admitted almost at once to the roomy hall where the earls received messengers and heard petitions, and Kata scarcely had time to look at the trestle tables and benches, and all the people sitting at them, and at the tapestries hanging on the walls, before a servant led them up to the high seats, where the new young Earl of Northumbria sat with his elder brother, Earl Edwin of Mercia.

"Wilfred," she heard Wilf saying. "Headman of Riccall."

"Excellent!" said Earl Morcar. "And you, girl?"

Kata swallowed, and Wilf nudged her.

"Lost your tongue?" asked the young earl.

"I'm Kata."

"Kata," repeated Morcar. "Strange name. Norwegian, are you?"

"Oh, no!" said Kata, and she felt shocked. "My mother was Edith. She was born in Riccall. Her husband was the headman, but he was killed by the Swedes and…"

"Now then," said Earl Edwin, ignoring her. He was several years older than his brother, and looked it – heavy-jowled, and rather ponderous. "Headman of Riccall. Why are you here?"

But no sooner had Wilf begun to explain why they had come than Earl Morcar held up his right hand. "I know!" he interrupted. "Our scouts shadowed Tostig when he sailed up to the Tyne and met Hardrada there. They've been shadowing Hardrada, too."

Earl Edwin nodded gravely. "They saw Scarborough burned to the ground."

"Burned!" exclaimed Kata. "What about the people?"

The headman covered his face with his hands.

"We've already sent messengers to our king," Earl Edwin told them. "Harold Godwinson."

"God be praised!" said Wilf. "God be praised."

Morcar shook his head and sighed. "But he and his army are three hundred miles away, on the south coast. Godwinson's afraid that Duke William of Normandy will invade us before winter comes."

"There's nothing for it," added Earl Edwin. "We've got to fend for ourselves."

"We aren't even certain Hardrada is heading for York," Earl Morcar said. "For all we know, he could be sailing south."

"Not if Tostig has anything to do with it," his brother said. He thumped the arm of his high seat. "He wants to reclaim his earldom. Your earldom, Morcar. He wants to reclaim Northumbria. We must all meet and meet at once. Our armed men, the citizens of York, the headmen from all the hundreds."

"I've already sent out messengers," Morcar added, "calling everyone to a meeting tomorrow morning."

"And I've told everyone to round up our livestock and be ready to lead them well away from the river," added Wilf.

"We must delay the Vikings," Earl Morcar said. "We must make things as difficult for them as we can."

"Tomorrow morning, then," Earl Edwin agreed. "We'll thrash things out. This is a meeting for headmen, and our lives depend on it."

The headman nodded and gestured to Kata. "She's trustworthy."

"No," said Earl Edwin.

"I am," Kata protested. "I am."

"She's a born leader," Wilf insisted. "Like her mother. I want her to learn. To see how people reach difficult decisions."

Kata looked at him, astonished.

"No," said the earl again.

"There's a hostel for pilgrims and wayfarers next to the chapel of Saint Olaf," Earl Morcar added. "She can wait there. The nuns will give you something to eat, and somewhere to sleep."

The nun carried a glowing candle into the dormitory.

"Seven pilgrims are staying with us," she told Wilf and Kata. "They haven't come back yet, but they won't bother you. They're quiet souls."

"Nun..." Kata began.

The nun smiled. "We say *Sister*. I'm Sister Innocenta. And our superior, we call *Mother*. Mother Bridget."

"Can I ask you something?"

"Of course."

"What's a bare sark?"

Sister Innocenta stared at Kata and burst out laughing. "Why? Where did you hear that?"

"One of the guards in Earl Morcar's fortress. He was telling another guard that some of the Vikings are bare sarks."

The nun laughed. "Well, now! I don't know. You'd better ask your headman."

"Oh!"

"Some people call them berserks, and they fight naked," Wilf explained. "That's what bare sark means. They worship the god Odin and work themselves into a frenzy, and in battle they howl, and leap, and bite on their shields."

"Holy Jesus!" exclaimed Sister Innocenta, throwing up her arms and pretending to be shocked.

"Yes, and protect themselves with magic spells and ointments," Wilf added.

Not Tor, thought Kata. Never! Howling and leaping... He can't be a bare sark. He can't!

"Well, now," Sister Innocenta told them. "Here's your bedding. Look! The covers are stuffed with eiderdown."

"What's that?" asked Kata.

"Feathers," said the headman. "Eider duck feathers."

"From Norway!" added the nun, and she laughed. "We can't be doing with any bare sarks around here."

CHAPTER 9

Slower than a heartbeat, and clean as a drop of clear water, a single bell chimed in the darkness. When Kata opened one eye, she was aware that shapes were stirring around her, and some of them were groaning.

Wilf was lying on the padding next to her. "You awake, girl?" he asked gruffly.

"No," said Kata, and she gave a prodigious yawn. "What is it?"

"The night service," Wilf told her.

By now the shapes around Kata and Wilf had turned into pilgrims, and they were on the move. They shuffled along a chill stone corridor to the nunnery chapel, and Kata and Wilf followed after them.

What awaited them fairly took Kata's breath away. The chapel was lit with yellowy candles, a few of them in iron candlesticks, a few up on stone ledges, and three times three on the altar, guarding the silver cross.

Dressed in their white habits, the nuns were standing in two long rows facing each other.

Kata grabbed Wilf's sleeve. "Look!" she exclaimed. "It's like ... like they're waiting to go to heaven."

"Shh!" said Wilf.

I could be like them, Kata thought. I could be a nun. Has God brought me here for a reason?

One nun walked up to the altar, and as soon as the pilgrims had sat down on two benches in the nave facing her, she began to intone in a voice that wasn't quite speaking but wasn't singing either.

It's Latin, Kata thought. I know it is because the words sound like Father Huw's. She sighed. I wish I could understand them, and if I were a nun, I could... But then Kata thought of Tor... She smiled a secret smile.

When she half-closed her heavy eyelids, everything in the chapel blurred. Like in a snowstorm, she thought. When the fields and the woods and the barn and everything become one breathing white ... spirit.

Now the nun raised her voice, and all the nuns repeated her words.

A furore Normanorum, libera nos, Domine!

Three times the nuns lifted their voices, and some of the pilgrims did too.

Wilf turned to Kata. "From the fury of the Vikings, deliver us, Lord!" he said.

"Amen!" replied Kata, rather more loudly than she'd meant to.

After this, the nuns proceeded in pairs out of the chapel

– all but two of them. Each with a silver snuffer on a long stick, they put out the flickering candles.

As soon as she got back to the dark dormitory, Kata lay down and pulled up her cover over her head. She tried to think about everything she had seen and heard in the chapel, and how even the nuns had prayed about the Vikings, but she was so tired that very soon she fell asleep.

Sometime before dawn, though, she had a horrible dream.

A circle of bare sarks had surrounded Tor – she was certain it was Tor, although she couldn't see him properly – and they were leaping up and down and yelling that he was a coward, and then she saw Oswald was their leader.

Kata tried to scream, but she couldn't make a sound. She thrashed and threshed inside her floppy bedcover, and it was a wonder she didn't split it and send all the eiderdown flying and fluttering like snow around the dormitory.

"It's all right, girl! It's all right!"

Wilf was sitting up on his padding.

"Terrible!" wailed Kata, and she buried her face in her hands.

"You got caught up inside that cover and couldn't get out."

Kata was still half trapped inside her dream when she and Wilf broke their fast with the other pilgrims. Milk. Cold porridge. And a handful of blackberries that the nuns had picked at dawn.

A nun walked up to the high desk at one end of the refectory and read something from the Books of Samuel about David and Uriah the Hittite and the Prophet Nathan. But Kata didn't know who they were, and her mind kept straying, first back to the terrifying berserks, and then to what she'd heard about Scarborough and everyone there being burned to death.

"Now, then!" Wilf reminded her as soon as the nun had finished her reading and said grace. "Remember what Earl Edwin said?"

"Yes! You're to come back first thing in the morning. You – not me." Kata blew out her pink cheeks and tossed her head.

"I did hope the earls would allow you to come," Wilf told her. "But, actually, you're well out of it. I know how these things go. There'll be wrangling and tangling and loud argument for hours. Anyhow, you haven't been here to York before and you're what … fifteen? You haven't even seen Coppergate." The headman spread his arms. "Coppergate! I've never seen anywhere like it. If I'd any choice, I'd be coming with you. You be careful, though."

"What do you mean?"

"You know – this is a big city, and there are all kinds of bad eggs and rotten apples. Pickpockets and worse."

Kata nodded and grabbed a handful of her chestnut hair. "I know how to look after myself," she said.

Then Wilf reached for his inner pocket, and the purse inside it. He took out three coins, carefully inspected them, and gave them to Kata.

"Three halfpennies," he said. "Get yourself something to eat and drink at midday," he told her. "And you can spend what's left over. All the headmen will be riding in now, and likely as not the talk will go on half the afternoon as well. I'll meet you where we stabled our ponies."

"When?" demanded Kata, still chafing at not being allowed to the meeting with the earls.

"At nones. The ninth hour. When Christ cried out and died. We must give ourselves time to get home before dark."

Just before Kata set off, a nun pattered down a small flight of steps. It was Sister Innocenta. "You're away to Coppergate."

Kata nodded.

"Well, Kata, a double goodbye to you!"

"Double?"

"Because it's a double saints' day! Saint Cyprian and Saint Euphemia. Now don't you go asking me who they were, because I don't know. Well, I do know Cyprian's flock loved him, but the Romans beheaded him. And no one here knows a thing about Euphemia, except the poor lass was thrown alive into a lion's cage."

Kata screwed up her eyes.

"Anyhow, if you ask me, it's the Romans who were the wild beasts," Sister Innocenta said, shaking her head and laughing at the same time, as if she were describing the pranks of naughty children. "But you haven't come here to listen to tales about saints – and the truth is most of them came to bad ends, didn't they now?"

"Will we?" Kata asked her. "I mean..."

The nun looked startled. "Will we what?"

"Come to bad ends?"

"What do you mean?"

"**The Vikings.**"

"Oh! I see," Sister Innocenta replied. "No, my dear. I don't think so. For all their sins, they're Christians – and I don't believe they'd ever attack a holy house. They'd never attack monks and nuns."

"But what about the rest of us?"

"My dear!" murmured the nun, and she put both arms around Kata. "You can come back here whenever you need to. Next time I can show you our scriptorium."

Kata drew in her breath. First it was just me, wondering about becoming a nun, but now this sister is saying I can come back, and she'll show me … whatever she said. I do like being here; it's so peaceful, so safe. And I like Sister Innocenta, too. But staying here… Well, it won't save Riccall, will it?

"How old are you now?" the nun asked her.

"Sixteen. Almost."

"Yes, and I'm nineteen."

"The same as Meghan!" exclaimed Kata.

"Who?"

"Oh! My pony."

The nun laughed. "Well, then! I'm only three years older than you. Your elder sister, that's what I am! And here I am, talking the top of the morning away. Mother Bridget's always telling me I talk too much. Come back, Kata, come back soon."

CHAPTER 10

Kata wasn't prepared for Coppergate.

How could she have expected such a shocking press of people, shoulder to shoulder, sidestepping and shoving and jostling?

Never in her life had she heard such a buzz of conversation, or so much whistling and shouting.

Nothing! Nothing in all her world at Riccall, where she had never seen more people in one place than her friends and neighbours gathered in the headman's barn for the harvest festival or at Yule, and never heard noise louder than a flock of hungry sheep or an army of geese or the thrashing of the watermill.

As Kata picked her way along the wide street, and explored passages on either side of it, she could hear people talking not only in her own language and languages she half understood — Swedish and Danish — but in tongues she had never heard in her life before. And again and again she kept hearing the same words – Vikings, and *fljota*, and Hardrada… Hardrada, *fljota*, Vikings.

"You can't be a Viking," she said out loud, thinking about Tor. "You can't be."

All the stalls with open doors, stacked with utensils, and cups, and bowls, and fabric, and jewellery! Bone and antler! Silver and gold!

There was one stall where a woman was selling hones for sharpening knives, scythes and sickles, and Kata wondered whether she could buy one for Wilf.

"The best," the woman told her. "Much the best. From Norway."

"Are you Norwegian?" Kata asked her.

The woman nodded. "Yes, most of us here are."

"Are you a Viking then?"

"Me a Viking? Are you mad? The last thing we want is the Vikings here. We all rub along all right, in York. Side by side. What we want is peace, so we can trade. That's what most Norwegians want."

Kata smiled to herself. So being Norwegian didn't make you a Viking then. "How much is this hone?" she asked.

"For your sweetheart, is it?"

"Oh no!" exclaimed Kata, blushing. "I haven't got one."

The Norwegian woman narrowed her eyes. "I can find you one," she offered. "A pretty girl like you."

Kata shook her head.

"No? This hone then. Seven pence."

"Seven!" yelped Kata. "I only got three."

The woman sighed.

"It's for our headman. Down in Riccall."

"Five pence."

Kata heaved her shoulders.

"Go on then," said the Norwegian woman. "Three pence. Take your pick."

Pipes! Pipes! Pan pipes, bone pipes!

Ankle boots!

Hooks, loops and pins!

"Come, see the goblin with four ears!"

"The green girl! Green all over."

Kata inspected just about every stall in Coppergate. But after a while the buzz got inside her head, and she just wanted to get away from the market, and to be alone. On her way out, she picked up an apple from a stall, and it was pulpy on one side.

"Here, love," said a man, holding out another apple. "A good one."

When Kata looked at him, he opened his arms.

"An apple for a kiss," he said.

Kata screwed up her eyes. "Go away!" she told him.

The man didn't go away. He lurched towards Kata.

Kata immediately turned on her right heel and hurried out of Coppergate towards the river. But when she lengthened her stride, the man lengthened his stride, and she could hear him right behind her.

Kata broke into a run, but the man started to run too, and then she remembered Wilf's warnings.

As soon as she neared the riverbank, Kata could feel the

fresh September air on her cheeks.

Faster, she thought. I can! Faster than any boy in Riccall.

Kata saw that there were two trading boats tied up no more than a couple of hundred yards ahead.

"Come here!" bawled the man right behind her, so close to her that she could hear him panting. "Come on, my beauty!"

Kata shouted out for help as she ran up to the first boat, but there was no one on deck. No one at all.

"Come on!" the man yelled.

"Help!" cried Kata as she neared the second boat. "Help!"

A young man, whittling a staff, was sitting on the capstan where the boat was secured, and at once he stood up and stepped straight between Kata and the man chasing her. He whacked the man across the face with his staff and felled him.

Kata stumbled onto her knees, gasping.

She turned round and looked at the man from the market grovelling on the ground. Then she looked up at her rescuer...

She saw his long, fair hair.

His bright blue eyes.

It was Tor.

CHAPTER 11

"I knew it!" exclaimed Tor. "I knew we'd see each other again."

He threw his staff sky high, and then bent down and grabbed the man who had been following Kata under his left shoulder and pulled him to his feet.

The man had a red welt across his right ear and cheek, and his nose was broken. "She's mine," he muttered.

"I'm not!" yelled Kata, and she jumped up. "I never seen him before in my life."

Tor picked up his staff. "You scum! Clear off!"

The man slowly turned away, then glared over his shoulder. "I'll be back," he said darkly.

"Your poor hands," Tor said after the man had gone. "Your poor knees."

Kata inspected them. "Always bleeding," she said. She smiled, but then she gave a sob.

Tor clenched his right fist. "I knew it! I did."

"What?"

"It's fate."

"What do you mean?"

"There are thousands of people here in York," Tor began. "Thousands and thousands. We have a saying—"

"So do we," said Kata brightly. "It's like looking for a pin in a haystack."

"Like that," Tor agreed. "And then I wondered ... I wondered ... well ... whether you might look for me. Like I've been looking for you."

Kata lowered her eyes.

He was looking for me, she thought. For me! He was. No one's done that before.

"I picked up my boat at the watermill early this morning. It's like I told Bullfrog, I got left behind, so I had to catch up with her."

A man appeared on the deck above them and leapt down onto the quay. "Ah! You've met my young friend already," he said. "Whoever you are."

"Me? I'm Kata."

"Well, Kata, here's a word of warning. Don't trust a word he says."

"Matason!" protested Tor.

"You jumped ship."

"I did not. You left before I could get back. You know that."

The skipper pursed his lips and smiled.

"As if I'd have left you with my pony," Tor said hotly.

Matason clicked his teeth. "That was part of our bargain."

Tor shook his head furiously.

"You can't trust him," the skipper said to Kata, "but he is very charming. Come aboard now. My wife, Safæ, she'll get you cleaned up. You too, you rogue!"

Tor strode over to his pony, Skopti, nuzzled him, and introduced him to Kata. And then, while they were sitting in the bows, Safæ wiped Kata's hands and knees with a damp cloth and then brought her husband and the two of them mugs of fresh apple juice. Before long, Tor and the skipper stopped needling each other, and for the first time since she'd left the hostel early that morning, Kata felt calm and safe.

She and Safæ began to talk about where each of them came from, and soon discovered that both their mothers had been slaves and had both died only months before.

"You staying with us?" Matason asked Kata.

"Oh no!" she replied. "No."

"You could," Tor told her.

"I can't. I'm meeting Wilf at the stables."

Matason raised his eyebrows. "Wilf?"

"Our headman at Riccall. We rode up here yesterday so he could talk to the two earls, and we've got to get home before nightfall. I'm meeting him at nones."

"Where?" Matason asked.

"You heathen!" Tor told him. "The ninth hour. The hour Jesus died on the cross."

"Of course!" said the skipper. "You'd better get a move on then."

Slowly and stiffly, rather reluctantly, Kata got to her feet, and Tor strode over to his pony, and slapped his neck twice.

"I'll be back," he promised him.

Then he and Kata stepped down onto the quay and they set off together along the riverbank.

I'm as tall as he is, Kata thought. Almost.

"What?" Tor asked her. "What are you thinking, Kata?"

"You've never said that before," she told him.

"What?"

"My name. I like the way you say it."

Tor laughed, and he looked at Kata with his bright blue eyes and scuffed the path. Kata could feel her right knee was bleeding again, and she felt so clumsy.

"Can I ask you something?" she said.

"Anything," Tor replied. "Everything!"

Kata stopped and looked Tor squarely in the eyes. "What's a Viking?"

"What do you mean?"

"I don't know exactly. Vikings are Norwegians, aren't they?"

"Yes."

"So are Norwegians Vikings?"

Tor laughed. "No, of course not. Vikings are raiders. Armed raiders. Summer raiders."

"With fleets and armies?"

"Sometimes, yes," said Tor. "Sometimes with just a few boats, a few dozen men. Most Vikings go back to their own families in Norway over winter, but some stay, and they settle here … and marry English girls." He gave Kata a sly smile.

Kata dipped her head. "Lots do in York," she said. "So are berserks Vikings?"

Tor guffawed.

"**Are you? Are you a berserk?**"

"Me?" Tor swept back his fair hair and laughed loudly. "I'm a fisherman from Orkney, like my father was. Like Eirik."

"Eirik?"

"My friend. He drowned on the boat from Orkney… Anyhow, how do you know about berserks?"

"A nun told me."

"A nun!" Tor laughed again.

"Don't laugh," Kata said. "Nuns are… I don't know…"

"You? You don't want to be a nun?"

Kata smiled and shook her head.

"I could come with you," Tor suggested.

"Where?"

"Riccall."

Kata shivered.

"I could," said Tor in a low voice.

Kata drew in her breath. She felt so confused. She didn't say anything.

"Why not?"

She stood on the spot, thinking of all the reasons why not, but also sensing what her body was telling her, and knowing how her head and heart were arguing furiously.

"Because…" she began. "Because the Vikings are coming."

"That's nothing to you or me," Tor protested.

"Nothing!" exclaimed Kata. "It's everything! Harald Hardrada. His fleet. We've got to prepare in case he comes. We've got to round up our animals and be ready to leave our homes. Yes … and … and everything."

"Well," said Tor after a while, "if I can't persuade you to let me come with you … I'll have to follow you."

As if some dark cloud had lifted inside her, as if she were bathed in sunshine, Kata turned and just brushed Tor's forearm with her left fingers, unconstrained and joyful.

"Have I been waiting to meet you all my life?" Tor exclaimed. "I'm going to find out."

CHAPTER 12

Riding back to Riccall, the headman and Kata had plenty to tell each other, but she kept her meeting with Tor a secret. She couldn't stop thinking about him. Would he really be as good as his word and come to Riccall?

"I've never heard so many words," Wilf complained. "So much argument. Everyone had to have his say." He kicked his pony into a trot. "I can't get it all straight in my own mind. Let's cover a mile or two to clear our heads, and then I'll tell you what's what."

So the two of them cantered all the way back to the loop in the river at Fulford Ings before they pulled up, breathless.

"Very good," said the headman.

"Wilf," exclaimed Kata, "look at the water meadows!"

He nodded. "They'll be completely flooded when all this rain has come down from the moors. Now, Kata, the long and short of it is this. The two earls fear the worst, but they really don't know where they stand. They need to find out how many Vikings there are. How many ships. How many men. Where they'll land. They've sent out scouts all over the place, and of course Snell and Rinan and Odda may have news for us by now."

"Bullfrog too," said Kata.

"Yes, the earls fear the worst," the headman said again, and gravely he shook his head. "They don't think they'd be able to defend the city, and if they can't..." Wilf shuddered. "And of course they know that all the Norwegians – you know, all the traders who've married and settled here... Well, they'll just keep their heads down and hope for the best."

"I know that!" exclaimed Kata. "In Coppergate, I kept hearing the last thing anyone wants is an invasion. And not all Norwegians are Vikings."

Tor isn't, she thought. I know he's not.

And it was as if ... as if she said it enough times, she could make it true.

"So the earls are going to assemble all the men they can, and as quickly as they can. Not just from York but from all the hundreds round about. And as soon as they hear the Vikings have disembarked, they'll march out of the city and take them on." Wilf paused, dropped his reins, and spread his arms wide. "The earls, they'll draw up somewhere around here," he added. "That's my guess."

Kata stared at the scrub to her left, and the boggy water meadows across the river, and the sweet water, now running so softly, ribbed with blood light from the lowering sun.

"Do they have to?" she asked.

"Have to?" said Wilf. "Have to what?"

"Fight." She shook her head. "This place is so peaceful. Why do we have to fight?"

"Well!" said the headman. "What about you? Coppergate?"

"Oh!" said Kata, and she shook her head.

"Spit it out."

"You know I told you about that Norwegian boy. The one I met with Oswald and Hilda. And you said, 'Norwegians behind us, Norwegians ahead of us', and something about a screech owl, and a warning."

Wilf pursed his lips and nodded.

"Well, the warning was sort of right! I didn't know what to expect. But I saw him again." Then Kata told the headman how Tor had helped her when a man had chased her as far as the river and the trading boats.

"Ah!" said Wilf.

"He said he might come back to Riccall before he goes home to Orkney."

"Ah!" Wilf said again. "Not to see you, of course!"

Kata dipped her head.

"Well, you must be sure to bring him to the village then," the headman added with a little smile.

By the time Kata and Wilf rode into Riccall, it was the blue hour, and almost everyone had already retreated into their huts and cottages, but while they were feeding their ponies in the paddock, someone pottered up to them.

It was old Kendra, the wise woman, stumbling along inside her woollen wrappings, layers of them – the ones she wore whatever the season. She was warbling to herself.

"Still up, Kendra?" said the headman.

"Hear it, did you?"

"What?"

"That old screech owl again. Perched on the barn."

"We've only just got back," Kata told her.

"Well," the headman said, "Kendra's the one – she's the one to ask about your screech owl!"

"Snell and Rinan and Odda just got back too," Kendra told him.

"Already!" said Wilf. "Right! I'll ask Father Huw to ring the summoning bell at cockcrow. We must all hear whatever they have to say."

The two fishermen and Odda stood with Wilf at the far end of the barn, and everyone perched on the bales around them. Outside, hundreds and hundreds of swallows were twittering and racing around, on the very point of leaving for somewhere far south.

"Well?" asked Wilf.

"Before, when you rode to York," Rinan began.

"Yes, the Vikings sailed south from Scarborough to Withernsea," Snell added.

"Yes, and they were attacked," Rinan said.

"Who was?" asked Kata.

"All of them."

"And there were seven ships…"

Kata smiled and she slapped her forehead. Neither Snell nor Rinan were anything like as skilled at catching words as they were at hooking or netting fish, and Odda hadn't said anything at all. Kata turned to Wilf.

"Wait a moment! Wait a moment!" said Wilf. "Let's sort this out."

And so, step by step, the headman and all the villagers learned that, after setting fire to Scarborough, Harald Hardrada had sailed south and been attacked by seven Saxon boats at Withernsea. The Saxons had managed to set fire to one warship before the Vikings drove them off, and chased them back to land, and killed them all.

"Forty-three men," Snell told everyone.

There was complete silence in the barn, but then to everyone's surprise, Snell, Odda and Rinan grinned at each other.

Kata screwed up her face and shook her head.

Then the three of them opened their mouths and bellowed:

"Harald, he's old, Harald's creaky.
Harald's mouldy and he's leaky."

Everyone in the room began to laugh.

"Harald's fifty-two, he's crawling with lice.
This is Hardrada's last throw of the dice."

All the villagers shouted in delight.

It's such a relief, thought Kata. Such a relief to laugh.

Wilf raised both hands. "Where did that come from?" he asked, shaking his head and laughing.

"Downriver, they're making scorn-songs," Rinan told everyone, "and they'll sink Hardrada." Then both fishermen waved their arms, and everyone in the barn roared the last two lines again, Kata as loudly as anyone.

"Harald's fifty-two, he's crawling with lice.
This is Hardrada's last throw of the dice."

"It's good to laugh," the headman called out. "Very good. But now we know for sure, we can be quite certain that Harald's not sailing south but heading straight for us."

CHAPTER 13

Harald Hardrada stalked up to the bows. He shielded his eyes against the setting sun and looked up the estuary of the River Humber, deep into England. For a while he stood silent, and then he walked over to his skalds, Arnor and Thjodolf, who were tossing a hagstone between them, and chanting:

"Override ... undermine ... overcome ... undertake ... overhasty ... undercut..."

The king stuck out his lower lip and nodded.

"Overeager ... undergo ... overreach ... underfoot ... overweening ... underlie ... overfall ... undertow..."

On they went, and half listening to them, Harald felt as

if they were somehow telling him all his own inner anxieties about sailing south to claim the English crown. He raised his right hand.

"You poets," the king told them. "You've come with me on many an expedition. There's always work for you."

Thjodolf nodded. "To foretell. To celebrate. To remember. So those who come after us will never forget."

"Sire, after you met Earl Tostig, I made this verse," Arnor told him.

"I'll hear it," replied the king.

"Paltry! At the mouth of the Tyne
Tostig met Harald with a mere seventeen ships,
but he promises to bring three thousand men
to share in the swordplay. 'Are his words
made of air?' Hardrada asked. 'Can I trust him?'
'I've often heard,' said his son Young Olaf,
'that Englishmen are always untrustworthy.'
'Two days wasted,' growled Hardrada.
'Loosen the sheets and let rip to Scarborough.'"

"Very good!" pronounced the king. "Well, Earl Tostig had better keep his word."

"And after we left Scarborough," Thjodolf said, "I made this verse, sire." He drew himself upright and closed his grey eyes.

"One hundred and one years ago
Skarthi the harelipped settled here.
Some people call it the place of the skull.

When flames fell from the sky,
Hardrada reclaimed it. Every building
in that settlement blazed and collapsed.
'Words spread like wildfire,' Hardrada said.
'Let Scarborough's fate serve as a warning.'"

"Yes," the king repeated loudly, "'words spread like wildfire.' Were those my words?"

"Almost, sire!" said Thjodolf with a half-smile.

"I made poems when I was young," Harald told them. "When I was a Varangian in Byzantium. Fierce and passionate. Yes ... but I got out of the way of it. So now you two speak for me."

Then Thjodolf dropped the hagstone, and Arnor laughed. "You're the underdog," he crowed. "I'm the overmaster."

"Last night," Harald told them, "I had a dream."

The two skalds stiffened.

"Not like the last one?" asked Thjodolf. "The one you had before we set sail from Orkney?"

The king stared away to the west again. Above the horizon stretched long bales of silk, quite floppy, blood-red and orange, curtaining the whole September sky. "That ogress with her crimson shield, and those eagles and ravens... No, this dream, was warning me to turn back, turn back before I fill England's graveyards with brave Vikings."

Arnor and Thjodolf knew better than to interrupt or argue when the king was in this dour mood.

"In my dream," Harald said darkly, "there was no shouting, no blood, no corpses. No! I met my brother, Olaf. My dead brother. We were in Trondheim."

The king paused until the last slice of the sun had sunk out of sight.

Overhead now, purple-grey clouds rolled into and over each other.

"We were alone," the king told his skalds. "Just the two of us. Standing on the quay. Olaf reminded me how many battles we'd won, and he told me that he'd known when to stop."

Harald paused.

"He knew when enough was enough," he added. "That's why he's revered all over Norway. I tried to answer him, but Olaf raised his right hand, and I was tongue-tied. 'My brother,' Olaf said to me. 'My dear brother. You've fought and won battles in Russia and Sicily and all over Scandinavia. You are Hardrada, you're the greatest of all the kings of Norway. But I fear for you now. I can see you're setting sail for your own dying day.'"

CHAPTER 14

Kata didn't have to wait long for Tor.

"Sweet Jesu!" she gasped when she saw him striding towards the great barn, swinging his staff to ward off the three foxhounds yelping and leaping around him. It was only just after midday on the day after she and Wilf had got back from York.

Kata dropped the sack of carrots slung over her right shoulder. She ran half a dozen steps towards Tor, then checked herself and waited.

"I told you," he called out.

"What?"

"I said I'd come."

Kata felt so happy. But she knew Oswald and Hilda were standing on the far side of the yard, watching, and Snell and Rinan were sitting on the log bench, watching, and Father Huw had just limped out of the vestry and…

"Where's your pony?" she asked Tor.

"Matason wouldn't let me bring him."

Kata's eyes were shining. "You walked all the way?"

Tor put his right hand over his heart. "For you."

"I know but ... but you've got passage in two days."

Tor stretched his arms as wide as the world.

Kata lowered her eyes. "No time," she said.

Tor slowly shook his head. "Long time," he replied.

Standing there, very still, in the heart of her own village, with the midday sun warming her back and lighting up Tor's long, fair hair, with the hounds chasing each other, and dozens of martins jostling on the ridge of the barn, and pairs of eyes watching her and watching over her, Kata felt as if she were somehow between times and between worlds. Between Riccall and the war wolves, between peace and war, between nothing changing and everything changing. She couldn't quite explain to herself what she meant.

"We're clearing out of the village. We're getting ready as fast as we can... The Vikings are coming. We think the Vikings will stop at Riccall on their way to York because the river is too narrow beyond here."

Tor nodded. "You must keep safe," he said. He took a single step towards her, then shook his head.

Kata brushed the corners of her eyes.

Tor quite gently laid one hand on Kata's folded arms, but she quickly stepped back. "No, you can't do that. Not here."

Tor nodded.

"The two earls have decided to make a stand against Hardrada outside the city. At Fulford. Fulford Gate.

Everyone agrees they can't defend York. Its walls are crumbling."

Then Kata saw the priest crossing the yard towards them.

"Father Huw," she told Tor, and she slightly wrinkled her nose. "He does talk."

"Tor," boomed the priest. "It is Tor, is it? Not Thor."

"Same name," Tor replied with a smile.

"Ah yes!" said Father Huw. "Yes! What's the word? Interchangeable. Like some of our saints and your old gods. Anyhow, our headman asked me to welcome you if you turned up. He's downriver."

Tor politely inclined his head.

"So you're a fisherman," Father Huw said.

Tor nodded.

"And Norwegian?"

"I live in Orkney now. My friend Eirik and me, we were out fishing when the wind got up – first a skuther, then a real cat-risper – and we were swept south, far south past the west coast of Scotland."

Father Huw nodded.

"We overturned, and Eirik was drowned…"

"So you worship Saint Cod, do you?"

Tor frowned, and Kata knew that Father Huw was teasing him.

"And Saint Mackerel, and those other salty saints?"

"No, sir. I'm Christian."

Father Huw smiled and nodded. "I'm glad to hear it. Saint Mullet? Saint Hake?"

Tor looked perplexed. "I've learned about your saints," he said. "Saint Cuthbert, Saint Bede."

Father Huw raised his eyebrows. "Have you, indeed?"

"Most Norwegians and Orkney men are Christian," Tor said earnestly. "Hardrada is Christian."

"But he seems to think it's all right to attack other Christians," Father Huw replied tartly. "Well, Tor, you're welcome here, even if there's a fleet following you."

Tor shook his head. "What do you mean? I'm going home to Orkney."

Kata was beginning to feel uneasy.

"Father," she said, "I want to show Tor everything. Will you walk round with us?"

Father Huw gave her a knowing look. "Be careful, Kata. Let God guide you."

As he walked round Riccall with Kata, Tor grew determined to spend more time with her. He liked her directness – the way she said what she thought. He liked her shyness. Her smile. Her long stride. Her strong will and dark eyes.

I'm not being disloyal, he thought. I'm not risking anything by doubling back to Riccall. It's the only way I can see more of her. The fleet won't be arriving yet. Not for a few days – so I can still honour all my duties.

Kata reached out in front of her and opened her arms. "This is my strip," she said proudly.

"Strip?"

"My earth. My land."

Tor shook his head. "We do not have this."

"Each of us has our own strip," Kata told him. "And we have to plough and crop it. And then we have fields we all share. Our cow field, and sheep pasture, and the pig run. That's our common land."

Tor shook his head again. "Not in Norway. I mean. I lived there until I was twelve," he said glibly, "before I went to Orkney."

"And some wheat and barley we have to give to the headman and Father Huw, and some we can keep for ourselves. It's the same with cabbages and parsnips and everything."

"And you carry the corn to Bullfrog," Tor added. "What about this strip here, next to yours?"

"Oswald's," Kata told him. "Yes, Oswald's."

Tor at once thought of the way Oswald had put his arm around Kata. "Messy!" he said. "His strip is messy."

Kata nodded.

"You like him?"

"What do you mean?"

At that moment Oswald himself came striding up to join them, followed by Eager who was doing his best to keep up with him.

"What are you doing?" Oswald called out. "Kata?"

"Admiring your strip."

"What?"

"Messy," Tor told him, grinning.

Oswald glanced at Tor. "Speak for yourself!" he said brusquely. "Do all you Norwegians and Orkney men groom your hair?"

Tor frowned and shook his head.

"And cut and paint your fingernails?" Oswald splayed his fingers and hung them out as though to dry in front of Tor's face. "That's what I've heard."

Eager laughed and copied him.

"Sissy!" said Oswald. "Know what that word means?"

Tor could feel the muscles in his neck tighten.

"Lost your tongue, have you?" Oswald said, and he spat on the ground and turned away.

"Come on," said Kata nervously. "I want to show you the church and our barn and the paddock and pens and everything."

But it seemed that everyone in the village wanted to meet their visitor, and each time they took a step forwards, they had to take two steps sideways, and Kata realized that Wilf's intention in welcoming Tor to the village was to enable her to see him through the eyes of all her friends and neighbours. There was so much Kata and Tor wanted to say to each other, and so much they could not.

"It wasn't a church to begin with," Kata explained as soon as they'd stepped through the little arched door. "That's what Father Huw told me."

"What was it then?"

"He doesn't exactly know. A serious place, he says."

"What do you mean?"

"A place for thinking about heaven and hell and everything, and praying."

"Maybe it's where people once prayed to the old gods," Tor suggested.

"Yes, like Woden for winning battles. And Freyja for good harvests."

"Like that," Tor agreed.

"And where they made blood sacrifices."

Tor stepped away from Kata and spread his arms. "How airy it is. And cool. Our church is made of wood, and it sort of closes you in, but this place opens you out."

The way he thinks things, Kata thought. I wish I could say things like that.

"I like this painting up here," said Tor. "Saint Mary and the angel. Ochre and sky blue. And Mary looks so glad."

"Because she has been chosen," said Kata. "Because she doesn't know what's going to happen."

"Yes," said Tor. "That's right."

"Father Huw told me it's sort of sunk into the limestone," Kata told him. "And it was brighter once."

She prowled around and then stooped to inspect something low on the wall, close to the door.

"What is it?" asked Tor.

"Look! This fish. With such a big tail. What kind is it?"

Instead of answering, Tor got down onto his knees to have a closer look, and for a moment the tops of their heads just touched, and each of them knew it. Kata drew back as if she had been scalded.

"A carving," she said quickly. "It's a carving. It's what people … what people … what they used to carve or draw, to show they were Christian." She felt quite flustered. "In the old days, when most people worshipped the old gods and tortured anyone who didn't."

"Is that what Father Huw says?"

But before Kata could reply, the door swung open, and Wilf shuffled in.

"This is our headman," Kata said. "Wilf, this is Tor."

Tor nodded, and at once offered to help Wilf and everyone in any way he could.

Wilf noted his sheer eagerness.

"When are you all leaving?" Tor asked him.

"As soon as we're ready. And you know why, I suppose?"

Tor lowered his head and gave a long sigh.

"Because of your countrymen," Wilf said fiercely, "burning down Scarborough ... on their way to attack York." He waved towards the moors. "There's a ruined village up there. Half the people died of the black plague. It's been deserted for almost fifty years."

"Poorhoe," added Kata.

"Know how to kill a sheep?" the headman asked Tor.

"I do," said Tor. "On my mother's farm."

"There's an elderly one," Wilf told him. "Poor old Annis! I don't think she'll make it. You and Oswald can kill her, and help Kata to skin and butcher her."

"She's so gentle," said Kata. "I rode on her when I was little."

"Right then!" the headman said. "Let's get a move on."

Oswald had already noosed old Annis and led her round from the sheep pen to the gravel pit where the villagers killed and butchered all their livestock.

"Where've you been?" he yelled as soon as he saw Kata and Tor. "Grooming your hair, were you?"

Tor frowned and clicked his tongue.

"In the church," said Kata.

"Norway!" jeered Oswald. "Orkney!"

He cleared his throat and hawked on the gravel. "Worthless! Bullies and bastards! Worthless!"

"Oswald!" protested Kata.

"I heard lots about you. Anyhow, what are you doing here?" Oswald waved his killing knife in front of Tor's nose. "Nosing round our village. Nosing round Kata! Father Huw says you're a spy."

Kata quaked. Surely, he didn't, she thought.

"Oswald!" she protested again. "No!"

"Not," said Tor.

"What then?"

Tor shrugged.

"Leave each other alone!" Kata insisted. "Both of you." She raised her hands.

But Oswald ignored her, and he stepped right up to Tor.

Tor held his ground.

Oswald narrowed his shoulders. "Clear off," he said in a low voice. He thrust his face right into Tor's. "We don't need you, and don't need your help. Me and Kata have killed sheep and pigs before, and we'll kill Annis here."

Tor's neck muscles trembled. They tightened. He raised his left fist and crashed it into Oswald's jaw.

"No!" cried Kata.

Oswald staggered sideways, and his killing knife sailed out of his hand, right across and out of the pit. He let go of Annis's lead.

"Right!" he growled.

"No!" pleaded Kata, and she stepped between them. "Don't!"

"Scum!" yelled Oswald. He launched himself at Tor, and

Tor unclenched his left fist and almost tore off Oswald's ear. Then Tor clawed and ripped Oswald's lower lip, and his bright blood spurted down into the gravel.

Backing off, then hurling themselves at each other again, down on their knees and dirty, wrestling on the biting gravel, Tor and Oswald fought. They fought, and Kata watched, angry and afraid, knowing that in a way they were fighting over her, but not only that. They were fighting because of the long hatred between the English and Norsemen and because of the terrible battle about to come. Kata wished, wished that neither of them would have to lose.

Then Oswald lowered his head, and he butted Tor fiercely just under his chin.

Tor lurched sideways, and Kata heard it. A horrible crunch as he fell to the ground.

Slowly Tor got to his knees, but his right arm hung, useless – the wrestling was over.

Oswald looked down at him. He kicked at the gravel, and little pieces showered all over Tor. "Get lost!" he gasped. "Never come back!"

Oswald turned his back on Tor and Kata. Stiffly he walked away. Old Annis, very carefully, she watched him go.

Kata dropped onto her knees, out of breath. She helped Tor to his feet, supported his right elbow, and slowly walked him back to her hut.

"Is it broken?" she asked. "I heard it. Is it?"

"I don't know."

"Old Kendra, she'll help."

Inside Kata's hut, Tor crawled into one corner. He curled up on the padding of fresh moss laced with sage and poppy that Kata had laid down only a few days before, and Kata knelt beside him.

Tor turned to the wall, and he sighed.

What now? thought Kata. What next? Will everyone be glad? Do they think I'm on Tor's side? Oh, I wish they hadn't fought.

CHAPTER 15

Tor was asleep when Kendra shuffled over to Kata's hut.

The wise woman narrowed her eyes. "Let's have a feel then," she said, and she carefully lowered herself and knelt beside him. With her ten fingers, she kneaded Tor's neck and his right shoulder and collarbone, and not even that woke Tor, although he did groan and shift.

"Lie still!" she told him. "Still as a stone." And then she looked up at Kata. "Wrenched!" she pronounced. "Torn. Not broken."

Kata closed her eyes and took a deep breath. "Praise be to God," she said.

"He's a strong one, isn't he? Let him rest and sleep. I'll mix some creams and make a sling for his arm."

"I can't just stay here," Kata told her. "Wilf needs all the help he can get."

"I know, I know!" snapped Kendra.

King Harald stood astride his dreaming son as if he were a corpse on a battlefield. "Well?" he boomed.

"Riccall, Father. Riccall. That's where to lay-up."

"Go on."

"You can't get further than the watermill there. Boats going upriver to York have to go through one by one."

"How far?"

"Ten miles, sire."

"Go on then."

"They're heading for the hills, the poor people in Riccall. Well out of harm's way."

The king snorted.

"The two earls are planning to march out of York to meet you."

"Are they, indeed? Why's that then?"

"I don't know, sire."

"Don't know!" Hardrada shouted. "You're here to know, aren't you?"

In his dream, Tor gasped.

"York's got huge walls, hasn't it?" demanded his father.

Tor cowered. "Maybe they don't think they'll be able to defend them."

"What else?"

"There are two traders tied up in dock, sire."

"So?"

"About to come downstream. Through the watermill."

"No!" snapped the king. "I'm not having that. Snarling things up. Getting in our waterway. Anything else?"

"I don't know, I don't know."

"Don't know? Who? What? Where? How many? When? That's what you're here for." Hardrada grunted and spat on the ground. "Well, Tor, it won't be long before we blood you."

"Sire?"

"Before you fight," boomed the king.

"I'm a scout, Father."

"And you're my son. When I unleash Land Ravager, you'll be right beside me."

"Sire … my wrenched…" Tor was growing more and more restless. He moaned and turned from side to side.

"I was fifteen when I fought at Stiklestad," his father replied, "and that Swede stuck his spear into my gut."

"I know, Father. Yes."

In the almost dark, Tor opened his eyes.

It was a dream, he thought. Only a dream. It seemed so real. Did my father say I'd have to fight? Beside him? I can't! I've never been trained. I won't. I won't betray Kata.

Tor could feel his heart hammering. Then he tried to sit up, and he yelped, and clutched his right shoulder.

Kata ducked her head and looked into her hut. "You're awake," she exclaimed.

"How long was I asleep?" asked Tor.

"Since yesterday. Yesterday afternoon. And now it's after midday."

Tor screwed up his eyes, opened them again, and yawned. "You're all spattered in blood."

"I know. One day mud, the next blood…"

"Yours?"

"No, no!" said Kata, and she inspected herself. "Poor old Annis. Two other pigs as well. One of them put up a fight."

Kata backed out of the hut, picked up her water bucket and poured the lot over herself. Then she came in again, wiping her face with her hands, and rubbing her hands on her smock. "Now! How's your shoulder?"

Very gingerly, Tor raised both shoulders and slowly relaxed them again. "I don't know," he said. "Very sore."

"Kendra came to see you," Kata told him. "She said it's not broken. It's wrenched and torn. Didn't you feel it when she buried her fingers in you?"

Tor clamped his left hand over his right shoulder and shook his head. "Dreams," he said.

"What about them?"

"Are they what's already happened, all mixed up? Or is it the other way around? Do things happen because you dream them?"

Kata shrugged.

"I can't make them out. It all seemed so real."

"What did?"

"Talking to my father. Telling him everything."

"About us?"

"Well, everything."

"I don't know," Kata replied. "I don't dream. I just lie down, and the next thing is, the cockerel's crowing." She knelt beside Tor. "I've been thinking. Thinking…"

"Well?"

Kata leant in close to Tor. "Can't you…?" she began.

"Can't you...?" And then, all in a hurry, "Can't you stay here a bit? You'll get work in York, easy as easy. Who says you've got to go back to Orkney?"

Tor shook his head. "I say," he told Kata. "I say so. And then on to Norway. I've got to help my old mother. She runs the farm and her hips ache, and she can't do it on her own. She's forty-six, you know."

Kata looked at her lap. "What's it like then, your farm?" she asked quietly.

Tor closed his eyes.

"What I see," he said. "These things. The green grass roof. And Shabby our goat up on it when he shouldn't be. I can feel the fresh wind springing over the hill and taste the blueberries we pick up near the top. I can smell the salt water in the fjord below. Oh, Kata, so much. So much." Tor opened his eyes. "And down by the jetty, the stones for my grandparents, and their parents, and the skipping, skapping... Is there such a word?"

"Slapping, you mean?"

"Slapping, yes. The water slapping."

"I wish I could see it," Kata said. "I do."

"You can."

Tor looked up. He gazed into Kata's eyes.

Kata blinked, and then smiled. "My place is here," she said.

At this moment, Old Kendra arrived, carrying a sling made of twisted honeysuckle strings and moss. She put down a small wooden bowl filled with lumpen grey cream.

Tor propped himself up on his good left elbow.

"I don't want anything that makes me sleepy," he told

her. "I've been asleep for long enough. And dreamed more than enough."

"Yes, Sir Tor! No, Sir Tor!" Kendra said tartly.

"Anyhow, I've got to head to York. Matason is leaving for Orkney, and I have to go with him."

"You can't," exclaimed Kata. "You can't go yet. Not with your crocked shoulder."

"I can," Tor declared. "Well … if you come too. Will you come to York with me?"

Kata drew in her breath. "Oh! I don't know."

The wise woman clicked her tongue, and Kata lowered her head. "There's so much to do here, and we're leaving for Poorhoe," she said, in a husky voice, staring at Kendra.

I could, Kata thought. I could go with him and all. I mean, we're not leaving for Poorhoe yet. Wilf, he'll be angry, but I can do what I like, can't I? I'm nearly sixteen.

"Well?" asked Tor.

CHAPTER 16

Meghan, Kata's Welsh pony, was as sturdy as her name, but she was nineteen years old, and quite unable to carry Kata and Tor at the same time.

"You're the one with the painful shoulder," said Kata. "I'll jog along beside you. After a while, we can change round."

How could anyone feel light-hearted, knowing the Viking fleet was sailing up the Ouse and only a day or two from Riccall, and that all the villagers were in great danger and would have to leave their homes the very next morning? But Kata felt free and joyous. Tor had wanted her to come with him to York. She had made her choice. They could be together for at least another afternoon.

And not only that, she thought. Despite the disapproval of old Kendra, and Hilda's mother, Mattie, and Father Huw and several other villagers, they would be alone together.

They followed the same route she and Wilf had taken just

three days before – past the Green Hills, along the riverbank to the hamlet at Cawood and on towards where it meets the River Wharfe, and narrows.

"Kata," said Tor. "In Norway we say a sunbeam for your thinking."

"That's lovely!" exclaimed Kata. "My thinking! Well, about being together, and seeing together, and hearing together."

"I know."

"That yellowhammer! He's been hopping along beside us for miles."

"Probably hungry," said Tor.

"Or else he's got something to tell us."

"You don't believe that, do you?"

Kata nodded. "Yes, I do. I believe birds sometimes talk to us. Some of us."

"If you were a bird—" Tor began.

"A missel thrush," said Kata. "They sing so sweetly. What about you?"

Tor shrugged.

"Come on."

"I don't know," he said. "Well, a mixture." He shook his head and sighed.

"You all right?" asked Kata.

"Sometimes words get in the way," Tor replied. Then he pulled up the reins and, carefully supporting his sling with his left hand, he slid off Meghan's back. "Let's change round."

"You all right?" Kata asked again.

Tor nodded. "Just wishing," he said.

It's his shoulder, thought Kata. Pain makes you feel so weary.

But as Tor lagged a little way behind Kata, he was thinking straight enough. He knew that all too soon he would have to make very painful choices.

I've told Kata that I'll be leaving with Matason soon, he thought. That's what Matason thinks too. But it's not true. I'm going to make my way downriver to my father and report to him.

I don't want to have to fight. How can I possibly fight the people Kata knows? And all the people in York, the English ones. They won't just submit. Never. They'll fight. So, what then? Bottle them up and slaughter them?

What do I want? What do I really want?

What I want is to be with Kata. Here, and then at home in Norway. Is there any way, any way at all, I could bring her back with me?

What am I to do? What am I to say to my father when I do meet him? What if I stay with Kata and never see him or Norway again? Could I really do that?

Tor gave a great sigh. I can't go with her to Poorhoe. That's impossible. Not with Oswald there. He'd turn everyone against me.

Play for time. I must play for time.

"All right!" he called out. "I agree! I agree! I'll stay in York until the spring."

"Oh!" exclaimed Kata. "Oh, Tor!"

Tor opened his eyes very wide. "You care for me," he said.

"I do," cried Kata. "I do."

And at that moment, she almost stepped into Tor's arms – but did not.

Soon it was Tor's turn to ride again, and within just a few minutes the first warehouses and sheds along the riverbank came into sight.

"I told Wilf," said Kata, "I told him I've never seen anything like so many before, and now I've seen them twice in three days."

"It's straight up the riverbank to Matason's boat," Tor told her. "I must tell him that I won't be going with him to Orkney. And I want to get Skopti back."

Kata shook her head. "I must stable Meghan. That place where Wilf and I did before."

"Good," said Tor. "Very good! That's the way."

First, they heard a hum. An insistent hum, as if the city of York were a huge hive for bees, not for humans. Then they heard a hubbub. And when Kata and Tor entered Earl Morcar's great courtyard, they saw it was seething with people. Earl Morcar's guards were lined up with overlapping shields along the front of his high wall.

For a few moments Kata listened to the demands and arguments and the yelling all around her.

"Everyone has heard the Vikings are very close," Kata said, "and they want to know what's going to happen."

"Of course."

"This courtyard," said Kata, "Well, this place is where

Earl Tostig lived until he was driven out."

"Driven out? What did he do?"

"He made us pay so much – such heavy tax – that many people starved. Wilf protested, and so did many other headmen. But it was no use. He was so uncaring. He cared only for himself. He was cruel. And the guards who tried to save him, they were all killed. Here in this courtyard."

"So where is he now then?" Tor asked, as if he did not know.

"Tostig? He was in Norway early this summer. That's what Wilf told us."

"Norway!"

"Yes, trying to persuade King Harald to attack us. He's promised King Harald Hardrada that he'll fight alongside him. That way he'll get his earldom back."

Kata was growing more and more flushed and upset, and when Tor tried to put his good arm round her, she brushed it off. Tor felt anxious. Did Kata know? Did she actually suspect that he knew much more about Harald and the Vikings than he was letting on?

"Come on!" she said, and she started to lead Meghan through the crowd to the stables. As she did so, she and Tor could hear snatches of conversation, filled with anger and uncertainty and fear.

"How near, did you say? How near?"

"Are we going to fight…?"

"Not us in the market…"

"No, outside the city. That's what I've heard…"

"Everyone!

"No, not everyone."

"No, the standing army…"

"Outside the city? Why?"

"The Vikings are strong at street fighting, not so strong in the field…"

"Who says?"

"They'll make demands first."

"Tostig. The rat!"

"What about the king? Godwinson? Is he on his way…?"

It took Kata and Tor some time to work their way clear of the scrum jostling around them, and all the while Tor guarded his right shoulder by resting his sling on Meghan's bent back.

"That building there," he said. "Is that a church?"

"Yes, the church of Saint Olaf."

"Olaf?"

"I think so. It was built when Norsemen ruled England."

And named for Olaf, our saint, thought Tor. Well, he's *my* saint! I've got his toenail here in my sea coat.

When Kata had stabled old Meghan, Tor said he would first walk through Coppergate and ask if anyone had seen or heard anything about the two boys from their own fjord, who had set out for England without paying his mother the money they owed her for all the amber she'd given them – and after that go down to the river and talk to Matason. I need to stop Matason and that other trader from leaving, Tor thought, remembering his dream. Harald said their boats would block his waterway. Perhaps I can find a boy to act as messenger for me…

Then Kata said that seeing the church had reminded her of the nuns. She longed to feel the peace of the convent again, and maybe see the scriptorium as Sister Innocenta had promised. "And I'll ask them about Saint Olaf," she added. "We can meet late afternoon at Matason's boat. After you've told him about staying here, and reclaimed your pony."

CHAPTER 17

Standing outside the solid oak door of the convent and the wayfarers' hostel, Kata could hear the shouting and hubbub in Earl Morcar's courtyard, and what sounded like the throbbing of a drum. She watched people running at full pelt away towards Coppergate, and a couple embracing, and a group of urchins playing tag. She saw and heard the world outside.

But inside the unlocked hostel door and thick stone walls, all this busyness, all these tides and small consolations were shut out. As if they had never been.

Kata picked up the little handbell standing on the bench beside the door. She shook it, shook it again, and held it to one ear as a nun pattered down a small flight of steps to greet her.

"Yes," said the nun, divining at once how her visitor was enchanted by the sweet tinkling of the bell and welcomed the stillness inside the hostel. "Yes, we call it without and within."

Kata slowly nodded.

"I think I know you, don't I?" the nun said. "Yes, of course I do. You're Kata."

Kata smiled. "And you're Sister Innocenta."

"You came back."

Kata swallowed. She felt like weeping. Everything within seemed so peaceful and straightforward, while the world without was so uncertain and dangerous, and yet ... yet so alive.

I want to be within, she thought, but I need to be without. Both.

Again, the nun read Kata's thoughts, and she sang a little ditty:

"What's without's without,
and often comes to naught.
Within's where head and heart
chime, and antiphons begin."

"What's antiphons?" asked Kata.

"Ah yes!" said Sister Innocenta. "It's when one half of a choir sings, and the other half waits, and then replies. We sing the psalms like that."

Kata nodded seriously, not sure that she fully understood.

"Well, Kata, welcome to you!"

"You said I could come back. I wanted to see the scriptorium. You told me about it last time."

Sister Innocenta smiled. She led Kata halfway up the

stone steps and then turned round. "Yes," she proclaimed with a gay laugh. "It's a grand place, so it is! This is where today meets tomorrow."

The scriptorium was at least twice the size of the church in Riccall, and as long and deep as all the little cells and chapel on the hostel's lower level.

Kata gazed up at the row of huge oak beams above her head; she inspected each of the walls, their higher halves built from well-cut limestone, their bottom halves panelled. And when she took a couple of steps forward, she saw the floor was made of timber too, and felt how springy it was beneath her feet.

Then she looked at the very long table in the middle of the room, and the one … two … three nuns bending over it. She didn't want to miss a thing.

"Come over here now," Sister Innocenta told her. "Come and meet my sisters."

Kata smiled shyly at the three nuns, and then drew in her breath as she looked down at the red deerskin stretched out on the table.

"Yes," said one of the nuns. "So beautiful. Feel it!"

Kata ran the tips of her fingers over the soft pelt.

"A huntsman brought her here only three days ago," Sister Innocenta told Kata. "A gift to God, he said. Here! You can see where his arrow pierced her."

"We've soaked her in lime and water," another nun told Kata. "Now we have to scrape away all her hair."

"What for?"

"That's the first step," Sister Innocenta explained. "Soaking the skin and scraping away her hair. Then we have to stretch her skin on that frame over there, see? And if there are any tears, we have to mend them. Then we shave and smooth the skin, and cut the pages, and—"

"Ah!" exclaimed Kata. "Father Huw, he's got a tiny little Mass book. He told me the pages are called vellum."

The nuns all smiled.

"That's right," said the first nun. "Vellum is the word for any kind of paper made from animal skins. But deer – red deer – this is the very best."

Sister Innocenta took Kata's right arm and guided her along the table. "And now," she said. "Look!"

One nun was preparing red and black ink and a second was mixing the white of an egg with tiny little threads, no larger than eyelashes. "Saffron," she told Kata. "It gleams. It's almost as bright as real gold."

Kata shook her head and smiled in wonder and delight.

"And every morning," the first nun said from the other end of the table, "we sharpen the goose quills – goose and swan – for our scribes with these penknives. Look! Sharp as sharp."

Kata was so absorbed by the work of the nuns at the long table that she hadn't even noticed the two scribes, each standing very still at their lecterns, and writing.

For a while, she watched them, enraptured.

"Without them," Sister Innocenta murmured, "where would we be?"

"Well," said Kata brightly, "we'd have to remember as much as we can. Like most of us do. I can't read but I do know all the words of Father Huw's services. In fact, I know them backwards." Kata gazed at the two scribes. *If I did* come here, she thought, if I did become a nun, would I be able to learn to read?

My mother told me that when she was forced to become a slave, the world opened up for her. She went to a jeweller's workshop and met a laughter-maker and sold furs and stuff to Bulgars.

So, would the world open up for me if I learned to read? I don't know, I don't…

I do really care for Tor, and he's going to stay in York and work here.

And just before she died, my mother told me to be sure to get married.

For some while Sister Innocenta had left Kata to her thoughts, but now she gently interrupted her. "Maybe you do," she said, "maybe you do know all the words of the services. But what about all the books of the Bible? And the teaching of Saint Augustine, and the other saints? And the thinking of Boethius?"

Kata shook her head and ran her hands through her hair.

Sister Innocenta laughed. "You look like an angel," she said. "A flying angel. And what about the warnings of Wulfstan, our own archbishop?"

"I heard about that," Kata told her. "Father Huw told us. How he warned us the Vikings would attack us unless we mended our ways. He said our world itself would come to an end."

"Yes," said the nun. "*The world is in haste, and it approaches the end.*"

"I wish I could read." Kata sighed, and for a while she and Sister Innocenta quietly stood behind the scribes and watched them. The only sound was the scratching of the points of their quills on the vellum, and one of the nuns sniffing.

"They get aches in their joints," Sister Innocenta said. "Especially their necks."

Kata nodded. "Like carrying sacks of corn."

"And you see those lines ruled across the vellum? They have to follow them, and make sure their lettering is all the same size."

"What if they do it wrong?"

"Each scribe has a wild boar's tooth, and if she needs to, she can scratch away the ink after it has dried." The nun paused. "Kata, think of the strain on their eyes. Copying all day in this dim light. Truly, our scribes are halfway to God."

"Amen," said Kata, and she folded her hands over her breast.

One of the nuns turned round and gave Kata a sweet smile. "Bless you!" she said.

"Sister," said Kata, "up here … up here it's like there's no time."

"Everything takes the time it takes," Sister Innocenta agreed. "When it's within."

Kata slowly nodded. "But time passes, too."

The young nun smiled. "That's why I told you that this place is where today meets tomorrow, and teaches tomorrow."

"I'm meeting my … well, my friend. We've got to ride back to Riccall."

"We'll still be here."

"What do you mean?"

"Like I told you. You can always come back."

Kata didn't quite know what to say.

"I understand," said Sister Innocenta, and she opened her arms. "Just now, your world outside is waiting for you."

"I wish…" Kata began. "Well, I wish I didn't need to go away. I wish I didn't have to choose."

"And I wish," said the nun, as she led Kata down the stone steps, "I wish I could persuade you to eat something before you go."

Kata shook her head.

"I'll get you a fist of bread from the kitchen, bread and a wedge of cheese, if our mice haven't already … communed with them!"

Sister Innocenta and Kata both laughed, and they embraced.

"My almost sister," the nun said softly. "Next time you come to see us, I hope you'll tell me about your family and everything."

CHAPTER 18

"**Where's Tor?**" demanded Matason. "And where are Razon and Mundir? Seal skins, hides, bloody sacks of whetstone. Damn them! We unloaded the whole lot ourselves, and now we've had to stow everything on our own – all those pots and leather scabbards, shoes, those spices and what have you. I'm the skipper, not a slave."

Matason angrily clumped down the short ladder into the hold to check that everything was shipshape, and so it was Safæ, giving Tor's pony a bucket of water, who spotted Kata swinging down the river path, followed by Meghan.

"Matty!" yelled Safæ. "Matason!"

The captain clambered up the ladder again. He lifted his chin and looked to high heaven. "In the nick of time," he said.

"Well, at least Tor's pony will have a companion," Safæ replied.

The skipper guided Kata and Meghan up the plank onto

the deck, and his wife at once took Meghan's lead and tied her up in the stern beside Tor's pony, Skopti.

"Look at them," she said. "They could be mother and son."

"Where's Tor?" Kata asked her. "Hasn't he got here yet?"

Matason's wife shook her head. "Matason says—"

"Matason can speak for himself," barked the skipper.

"He'll be here very soon," Kata told them. "I know he will. He came with me to Earl Morcar's hall. Then I went to the nuns' hostel, and we agreed to meet here late afternoon."

Matason grunted. "I want to get going."

"Get going?"

"Soon as we can. Under way. The Vikings are just downstream, and I don't want to be here when they arrive."

Safæ pointed down the riverbank. "Look!" she exclaimed. "Here he comes."

Tor was hurrying along the path, and he bounced straight up the landing plank onto Matason's trader, clutching his shoulder.

"Tor," said Safæ. "You're hurt. Catch your breath."

"Where have you been?" asked Kata.

Tor rubbed his neck. "I was looking for those two boys, the ones I told you about."

Kata shook her head. "Your shoulder… Is it hurting?"

Tor took a deep breath and very slowly breathed out again. "That's better," he said. "But no one had heard of them."

Tor took another deep breath, sat down on a barrel, and put his left hand under his sling. He hunched his right shoulder. "I got hurt," he said.

There's something else, thought Kata. Something Tor's not saying. I know there is.

Safæ looked along the towpath. "Now who's this?" she asked.

"Who's who?" the captain replied.

"A young man. He's in a high hurry."

A lad of twelve or thirteen – rather younger than Tor – ran up to the bottom of the gang plank. "Matason!" he shouted. "I'm looking for Matason."

"Tell him to come aboard," Matason instructed his wife. "I don't know. First, we were one too few, now we're two too many."

Matason swivelled round and looked at Tor. "Ever seen him before?"

Tor hunched his shoulders and shrugged. "No," he said. "Never."

The skipper stared at the lad. "Well, do you want passage to Orkney as well?

"Where?" said the boy.

"Never mind," said Matason. "Well, who are you then?"

"A messenger."

"From?"

"I must not say."

"From Earl Morcar? Tostig? Hardrada?"

The lad shook his head. "I must only say what I was told to say."

"And what," asked the skipper in an acid voice, "is that?"

Kata turned to Tor. "Is he Norwegian?"

"How would I know?" Tor replied rather sharply. "I don't know – in the market, half the people are talking English Norwegian and the other half Norwegian English." Then he bowed his head and stared at his feet.

"I bring you this warning," said the lad. "On pain of death, you and the other traders are not to leave your moorings in York. We need you in York."

"We," roared Matason. "Who is *we*?"

Tor's hiding something, Kata thought. I'm certain he is. I'm sure he knows who this message is from.

"I must not say," the lad repeated, and he glanced very quickly at Tor and then at Kata and Safæ. "I only say what I was told to say."

"Is that all?" the skipper demanded.

"Yes, sir."

"Right!" said Matason in a stony voice. "Get off my boat!"

The young lad inclined his head. "I will warn the other trader," he said. And then he walked away down the gang plank.

Matason strode up to the bows and slapped Skopti and Meghan on the rump. Then he rounded on his wife and Tor and Kata. "Well," he called out. "What did you make of that?"

None of them answered.

"You, Tor. You're never at a loss for words."

"I don't know," Tor replied.

"Speak up!"

"Well," Tor replied carefully, "it depends. If the warning is from Earl Morcar, he may think trader vessels are safe places to hold and imprison Hardrada and the Viking leaders. And if it's from the Vikings, they may think they could imprison the two earls here."

Matason tugged his beard. "So, they're both saying the same thing, you mean."

"In a way, yes. Or the Vikings may not want you blocking up their waterways."

"I get it!" snapped the skipper. "And you've never seen him before – that lad?"

"You asked me that before."

Yes, he did, thought Kata. And Tor said, *No* and *Never*.

Kata wrinkled up her nose and looked at Tor anxiously. He knew that boy, she thought. I'm sure he did.

Matason sighed. "I'll talk to the other skipper."

"And stay put?" Tor asked.

Matason tugged his red beard.

"Or leave tomorrow?" asked Tor. "Tomorrow afternoon?"

"I don't know! You heard what the lad said."

"I've been thinking," said Tor quite airily. "I may not go to Orkney after all."

"What?" exclaimed the skipper.

"No, not yet," Tor said, and he looked straight at Kata.

Kata's heart leapt. His eyes were so blue. She wanted to clutch his hand but held back. Yes, he's staying, she thought. He's keeping his word and staying. At least until the spring.

As Kata and Tor rode out of York side by side, neither said anything much for quite some way. Tor was grumpy because, to begin with, Matason had refused to give up his pony. "It's payment," he'd said. "That's what we agreed."

But then Safæ had intervened. "Go on!" she urged the skipper, and she tossed her long, dark hair. "It matters to him much more than to you."

Kata felt quite breathless and was thinking hard. I keep

wondering whether maybe, Tor is actually a scout. A Viking scout. Was that story true, about meeting those boys and getting them to pay for his mother's amber? And did he know that lad who came to warn Matason? Tor never spoke to him. What if he had met him before? I think Matason suspected that, and I wondered too.

I can't work it out.

Is he a Viking?

If he is, I've told him all sorts of things I shouldn't have done. Yes, what Wilf told me about the earls' plans, and about us going to Poorhoe, and leaving tomorrow. And he heard all the arguing in the courtyard of the residence, and everyone fearful…

Even if he is a Viking, that still doesn't mean Tor doesn't care for me. He does. I know he does. And what he told me about wanting to find out … about us … about what we could be to each other. It's the same for me. I care for him, too.

Before they reached Riccall, Kata and Tor were riding by the soft light of the moon. Away north, there were banks of dark cloud, but overhead the first stars winked and quivered.

Kata and Tor dismounted and rewarded their ponies with hay and water for all the miles they had covered.

"There's so much…" began Kata.

"I know."

"I mean, we've scarcely talked about anything. Anything at all. For miles and miles."

Tor looked into her eyes. "Don't fear," he said.

"I do. Well, I do a bit. There's so much I don't know."

Tor nodded. "We must trust, Kata. That's what old wives say. Know when to trust and when not to."

"My mother!" replied Kata.

"What?"

"She'd say that."

"I don't even know who she was, your mother. She's not in Riccall?"

Kata screwed up her face. Then she rubbed her eyes. "No, no! Edith, she died in June. She died before she could tell me all her stories, about how she was captured by a Swedish raiding party. Captured from Riccall. Before I was born."

"No," said Tor.

"And sold. Sold as a slave."

"A slave?"

"Yes, to the skipper of a trading ship. And she went all the way through to Russia to Kiev, and the Black Sea. She was a slave, but also his mistress, the same as Safæ. But then…"

Tenderly, Tor laid one hand on Kata's left shoulder. "Your father?"

"Oh no! Not him." Kata shrugged. "She never told me."

"Not some man in the village?"

Kata drew in her breath. "Oh no! No! I don't know really." She patted Meghan. "And what about your father? What about him? You've never told me."

Tor nodded. "Well," he said, "he and my mother don't live together. They never have. But I do see him sometimes."

Kata nodded.

"He's a landowner. A warrior."

"You mean a Viking?"

Tor didn't answer. Instead, he added, "I've got two half-brothers as well."

Tor knew he was telling Kata less than half the story, and he wished he were not. His heart lumped inside his chest, and he wished so much he could tell her everything.

Then both of them fell silent. It was so balmy. So forgiving a night. As if the place were listening to itself.

CHAPTER 19

Back in her hut, Kata helped Tor to duck out of his sling, and then she rubbed more of the sluggish ointment that Kendra had left with her into his shoulder.

Kata was weary after jogging and riding all the way to York and back, learning so much from the nuns in the scriptorium, and then talking to Matason. But above all she was wearied by her growing feelings for Tor. Caring about somebody makes you more alive and more tired, she thought. Both.

"You can sleep on my bedding," she told Tor. "It'll be more comfortable for your shoulder. I'll tuck myself into the footing outside. It's a quiet night." Then she stepped towards Tor, just leant gently into him for a moment, and turned away.

But sometime during the night, the wind picked up from the north and swept away the calm of the previous evening. And it began to rain. Soft drops at first, cradling Riccall, but soon quickening into hissing, insistent bursts.

All the same Kata heard none of it. And when at last she stirred, well after the cockerel had given up trying to rouse her, she lay listening to the patter of the rain falling onto the overhanging thatch, and felt the cool air on her brow, her left wrist. She yawned, stretched, and reached towards the entrance to her hut.

"Tor," she murmured. And then more loudly, "Tor."

Tor wasn't there.

Bundled inside the sea coat he had retrieved from *Mævill*, Tor walked in the half-light through sleeping Riccall to the riverbank.

For a long while he stared downstream, upstream, downstream.

Nothing.

Nothing but a pair of ducks dabbling, and the lily-pads swaying, and the river itself, pricked and pierced all over and shivering in the falling rain.

She's so quick, he thought. So orderly. The way she looks after me. And so – well, so shapely. But very soon Harald will be here, and what will I do then?

"What am I to do?" he said out loud. "Things are getting more and more difficult."

Tor looked downstream again.

I'll go and see Bullfrog at the watermill, he thought. He hates the Vikings. Clogging up the river and stopping the trading boats and their payments. I wonder what he's planning to do.

So Tor set off along the sticky river path towards the mill.

Somehow the rain brought his greasy sheepskin back to life. It smelt thick and familiar and reassuring, and Tor fondled the little bone box sewn into one of the corners.

Then he heard a terrible clanking ahead of him and quickened his step.

Puffing out his pink cheeks and exploding blasts of hot air, Bullfrog was smashing an iron crowbar against the mill wheel. Again and again.

"Cracked!" he yelled as soon as he saw Tor. "I've cracked it. Your mates aren't having an ounce of flour milled by me."

Tor shook his head. "They're not my mates."

"Bloody Vikings!"

"I'll help you," said Tor.

"What, with your crocked shoulder?" Bullfrog spat at Tor's feet. "I told Kata not to let you become her millstone. A millstone round her neck!"

"I'm not!" Tor protested.

"Oh?" jeered the mill owner, and he gave Tor a grim, sideways smile. "You're welcome in Riccall, are you?"

"Are you staying down here or going up to Poorhoe?" asked Tor.

"Nah! Plenty of folk round here bring me their corn. They'll make room for me." Then Bullfrog swung his crowbar again and gave the mill wheel another whack. "Bloody Vikings!" he cursed again. "We've had years and years of peace in these parts. Nineteen years. Since the Swedes came."

"Kata told me," said Tor.

Bullfrog glared at him. "Kata! Kata!" he scoffed, and he bared his teeth.

"Watch it," said Tor, backing away.

But Bullfrog had no intention of watching it! He roared, and raised his crowbar, and swung it at Tor.

"No!" shouted Tor. And he turned and ran for his life.

"The bloody Swedes killed my father," the mill owner yelled after him, "and his father too. They took away Kata's mother and they sold her. Now it's the Vikings!"

Kata tossed her head.

"You had no right to ride off," said Wilf angrily. "No right. What do you think you were doing?"

Kata blinked – she blinked several times. Wilf had never once spoken to her so harshly.

"How dare you?" Wilf demanded. "It's not just what you did. What will you do next? I need everyone here, everyone ready."

"I am! I am! And Tor, he's ready to help."

"This is no place for him now," the headman retorted. "You know that."

"But…"

"No time for dawdling and dandling."

"We're not." Kata looked Wilf squarely in the eye.

"I know you care for him. But that's not for now. No, Kata. Tell him to come back when…" The headman waved his arms. "I don't know when."

While Kata and Wilf were still standing outside the hut,

Snell hurried up the river path into the courtyard and made straight for them.

"Well?" demanded the headman.

"Yes," Snell called out. "The first Viking ships, they're less than seven miles downstream and closing in on us. They'll be here by midday!"

"Right!" said Wilf. "That's it. We must all leave now. Straight away, whether we're ready or not. Kata – you find Father Huw. Tell him to ring the bell. Tell him to thresh it."

Kata dived into the church.

The priest wasn't there.

She glanced up at the painting on the east wall, the one in which Jesus was walking on water, and his disciple Peter was stepping out of a fishing boat to join him, stepping right out onto the water before the wind got up and he became afraid.

I know what the words say, she thought. Peter calls out, "Lord, save me!" And Jesus says, "You of little faith, why did you doubt?" Yes, I know those words, because Father Huw told me, but I wish I could read them for myself.

But how can we have faith, even a little faith, when hundreds and hundreds of Viking ships are sailing up our river? How can we, when the Swedes raided Riccall and took away my mother and murdered her husband?

Then Kata scaled the ladder onto the wooden platform at the west end of the church, unhooked the bell, and started to ring it herself. Each time she pulled the rope, the bell rang and the rope fairly leapt upwards again, chafing and scalding her hands, and straining her shoulders.

When Father Huw heard the bell, he limped back to the church, and as soon as he'd taken over from Kata, she ran back through the misty rain to her hut.

The door was open, and Tor was already there.

"Where were you?" she demanded. "Where have you been? I woke up and—"

"I know, I know," said Tor. "I went to see Bullfrog."

"Snell says the first ships will be here by midday."

"Midday! Today?"

"We've all got to leave."

Tor looked at Kata and screwed up his eyes. He covered his whole face.

"Oh, Tor!" exclaimed Kata. "What are you going to do?"

"I don't know." Tor hesitated. "I can't come with you."

"That's what Wilf says."

"And Bullfrog took a swing at me."

"What do you mean?"

"With his crowbar. He's mad with rage."

"Why?"

"Because … because the Viking fleet's coming, and I'm Norwegian too."

"But you're not a Viking."

"No! No! I've told you I'm not."

"Oh, Tor!"

"Anyhow, he can't stay at the mill, and so he's smashed his own mill wheel."

"Oh no!"

"I think…" Tor began. "I should have stayed in York last night, but I wanted to be with you. Each hour together, it's so precious."

"Oh, Tor!"

"I think I'd better ride back to York. Yes … yes … that's

what I'll do. I'll wait to see what the earls decide."

Kata gave him a bleak little smile.

"I mean, what else can I do? Matason will give me shelter, but he's a prisoner himself now. He's not allowed to leave the dock. He's angry with me, I know, but I think he'll protect me."

Kata shook her head, and she clenched her fists.

"Whatever I do," said Tor, and he took hold of Kata's left fist, and opened it, and pressed her fingers gently between both hands, "I'll ride up to Poorhoe as soon as I can."

"But Wilf…"

"I know. But I will!"

"Oh, Tor! Promise me! Promise me you will. I don't care what Wilf says. I want you to come."

"I promise. Not tomorrow. You'll be so busy, and Wilf will need your help all over the place. Me getting in the way will only make him angrier. You'll all be at … sixes and sevens, that's what we say."

"So do we," said Kata, smiling.

"The next day then."

Kata could see how uncertain and nervous he was.

Tor widened his blue eyes. "I promise," he said. "I promise you, Kata."

CHAPTER 20

Oh! As many times as he had seen them before, Tor never tired of watching and marvelling at the way warships moved, seventy-foot long or even a little more, dancing down a fjord, bucking as they crossed the bar, sailing out south, and here and now, gliding upriver. Almost three hundred of them. Three hundred!

Squatting with his back to a weeping willow, wrapped in the sea coat that protected him from most of the rainwater streaming down the trunk and dripping from the higher branches, Tor watched…

He watched how the oarsmen in the first pair of Viking vessels shipped their long oars and came to rest alongside the bank just below him and the far bank, opposite one another.

They're water snakes, Tor thought. Shrithing sea dragons.

Over on the far side of the river, a man shouted out,

"Deserted! Abandoned!"

"What did you expect?" called the helmsman just below Tor. "A welcoming party?"

In the green shade, Tor kept still. Very still.

"Karl's men are going ashore as soon as they've tied up," the man on the far bank shouted. "Searching for supper."

"No fewer than five men. Remember what Hardrada said," the helmsman called out. "Nasty surprises. That's what he told us. We've got enough food here. The last of the smoked duck from Scarborough!"

"Yeah!"

"And ale too! A full barrel."

While the two men were still calling out to each other, the longships behind them were nosing forward in pairs, and taking up their positions immediately astern. When Tor cautiously stood up, he could see they already stretched well down both sides of the river.

Ten oars on either side, thought Tor, two men at each oar...

"See you later, mate," shouted the man from across the river. "We're going to be cut off!"

Then two more ships glided into position abreast the foremost pair of ships, and another two beside them, so six ships were straddling the river with only a small space in the middle between them.

Shouts and curses as the oarsmen shipped their oars! Wild flapping as they bundled their sails. Hurled ropes as they secured their boats.

Then a smaller craft altogether, a dinghy, manned by just a dozen men, worked its way into the gap between the three ships on the far bank and the three ships on the near bank.

More shouts! More curses!

The men on the dinghy secured their boat to the ships on either side of her, and very soon, all down the river behind them, the Viking ships and dinghies were doing exactly the same. So that was that! They had bridged the Ouse and were able to walk across from one side to the other.

"*Skedaddle!* That's what I told him on the cliff above Scarborough. *Skedaddle! I'll see you at the gates of York.*"

Young Olaf smiled at his father.

Harald Hardrada thumped the bulwark.

"He's sharp. He never misses anything. *You can be my eyes,* I told him."

"He's fly," said Young Olaf. "A chancer. You know he is."

Hardrada grimaced. "What are you smiling about?"

"He always suits himself first."

"You don't like him, do you?"

"Not much."

"He's got a good heart," said Hardrada. "He's growing into a fine young man. That's what I think. Anyhow, I've sent out plenty more scouts – at least a dozen pairs. But I want to give him a chance."

"Third sons," Young Olaf said testily. "They're always favourites."

"That's not true," Hardrada replied. "Anyhow, as you know full well, he's not even your mother's son."

Olaf shrugged. "A farm lad, really."

"Well," said the king, rubbing his bushy eyebrows,

"I could do with his company now. He does make me laugh. And he makes me remember ... faraway places, earlier times."

Young Olaf shook his head.

"His mother, Solveig, she saved my life, you know. And she nursed me for months. And then we met again, down in Byzantium... One grey eye, one violet... Yes."

"You're growing old," Young Olaf said.

Hardrada thumped the bulwark again. "I am," he said. "Fifty-two. Most men of my age are rotting in their graves." He sighed and shook his head. "The gates of York. We should be there in two days. Two or three."

"And Earl Tostig?" asked Young Olaf. "Will he be there too?"

Harald snorted. "He's promised to sail up here right behind us. But I've never really trusted him, you know that. It wouldn't surprise me if he turned up with Edwin and Morcar on either side of him."

"What do you mean?"

"And fought against us."

For a long while, Tor remained under the weeping willow, now and then cautiously stretching out his legs and flexing his toes.

He listened, how he listened, and how he watched as the Viking oarsmen began to clamber from ship to ship, carrying tents and equipment, until they were able to disembark and stretch their legs on the far bank.

Still sitting, Tor levered himself well back from the willow. Then stiffly he stood up and hurried along the path to the deserted village. He strode into the barn, picked up his pony's tackle and saddle, and walked round to the paddock.

Everything was just as it had been the previous day. Skopti, munching hay, was neither pleased nor bothered to see Tor, even when Tor greeted him and slapped his neck. A green woodpecker watched nervously from her perch on one of the harvest dolls made by Kata and Hilda. A rat smelt danger and bolted out of the barn.

And yet nothing was the same, and most likely never would be again. Tor knew that.

Because his right shoulder was still very sore, he had some difficulty in mounting his pony. Then, giving the warships and their crews a wide berth, he set off at once through the green gloom for York.

How strange, he thought, how very strange to be within hailing distance of my father, and yet to be turning my back on him. But I can't meet him yet, I can't. I've nothing much to tell him. And he might want to conscript me into his army. Anyway, he's not expecting to see me before he gets to York. The gates of York! That's what we agreed.

He'd ask about my sling. Well, I could tell him it was when Bullfrog took a swing at me ... and tell him about the broken mill wheel too.

But listening to those skippers, calling out to each other... Buckling down. Knuckling down. Getting ready, eager, for action. I don't belong here.

I don't want to have to fight. That's why I didn't really mind when my father said he'd chosen me as a scout. He told me as if he were promoting me, but I think that, really, he was elbowing me to one side. I'm sure that when he told them, my half-brothers, Magnus and Young Olaf, would have been scornful, but it's different for them. They've both been trained to fight.

I don't want to fight. It's not that I'm afraid. But when my father torched Scarborough – I felt as if he were wounding me. And here it's worse. Much worse. I'd never fight Wilf. Or anyone else in Riccall. Not even Oswald!

Where do I belong? Not with those skippers, and our Viking army. Not with the Saxons. Half of them must hate us as much as Bullfrog does. But not with Kata either. Not yet. Not until after whatever's going to happen does happen.

Where do I belong?

As Tor rode upriver, a bilious mist was hanging over the water and spreading over the wetland on either side of it. It rose and dipped and rose, and it enveloped him. He could see no more than a few yards ahead. But what he could hear were voices, and clopping, clopping.

Tor wasn't the only one putting distance between himself and the Viking fleet. From farms and hamlets all around, horsemen and horsewomen were hurrying towards some safety, safety in numbers inside the thick walls of York.

Quite suddenly, Tor realized that two horses were bearing down on him, both a good deal larger than Skopti, and two men were astride them, both with gleaming knives.

Still holding his reins, Tor held up his hands. "Whoa!" he exclaimed. "Watch it! Whoa! Who are you?"

"I recognize that voice," said one of the young men. "I do, don't I?"

"So do I," his companion said.

"It's Tor. Tor, isn't it?"

Tor peered at the two young men through the swirling mist. "Who are you?" he demanded.

Neither of the young men replied.

"Who are you, I said."

"Eirik's brother. Arni!"

"No!" gasped Tor. "Arni!"

"And me, I'm Bard," said his companion. "You know me."

"Where's Eirik then?" Arni asked. "I thought you were working together."

So there, in the sopping mist of that September evening, Tor explained what had happened – and how he and Eirik had been waterlogged and capsized and...

Arni leant forward. He buried his face in his horse's mane.

For a while the three of them sat together in silence, then Tor told them how he had buried Eirik, close by the sea, and how he planned to return there and raise a stone for him.

"I'll come," said Arni quietly. And then, much more fiercely, "Yes! Of course I'll come with you."

"But where are you going now?" Bard asked Tor. "I mean, aren't you going the wrong way?"

"Wrong way?" said Tor.

"We're riding downriver," Arni told Tor. "To find Hardrada and tell him that everyone's up in arms in the city. Tomorrow or the next day, the earls will be on the move."

"You'll find the fleet at Riccall," Tor replied. "I've been there all day. Watching all the tying up. Disembarking. Pitching tents. And now I'm taking news, urgent news, to two trading ships."

It's so easy, thought Tor. Lying. But I don't like it; I don't like myself.

"What trading ships?" asked Bard.

"In York. At the dock. I've got a message for the skippers that they're not to leave. They're not to leave whatever happens."

Tor spurred his pony. "I'll see you at the gates of York," he called out over his right shoulder.

CHAPTER 21

Time plays tricks.

Up in Poorhoe, not far below the weltering clouds, Kata saw that there was a very great deal to do. Mending thatches, repairing firepits and fencing and sheep pens, rebuilding stone walling – so much had rotted or collapsed since the villagers, stricken by plague, had abandoned the place fifty years before.

But after leading their livestock from Riccall to Poorhoe and wheeling three rickety carts uphill for most of the way – one heavy with salted carcases, one piled with vegetables and fruit, and one bearing Father Huw and Kendra and little Bliss, none of whom could walk far – everybody felt worn out.

For much of the time, Kata kept herself to herself, and when she did talk to Hilda or Ellette or anyone else, they could see she was living in two worlds.

I've ridden to York twice, she thought. Twice! I've seen the wonderful scriptorium in the hostel, and Sister Innocenta told me I could always go back.

But ... do I really want to be a nun?

What about Tor? My mind, my blood, they're alive for him.

Up here, though, it almost feels as if none of this has happened – all these changes and hopes and maybes. It feels as if I might never even see him again.

Wilf had surveyed the wrecked hamlet on his own, and then he called everyone together to discuss and decide who should stay where.

He always listens to us, thought Kata. That's why he's such a good headman.

"We must help each other," said Wilf, "and work together. I've no idea when we'll be able, or whether we'll be able, to go home... But not before Christmas, surely. For all I know, the Vikings have already burned down our barn."

The villagers hung their heads. They said nothing. Kata put her right hand over her heart and screwed up her eyes.

"I really know little more than you," Wilf told them. "We all believe the Viking warships will tie up at Riccall, and Hardrada's army will encamp there. Thousands of them. Thousands. In their tents, no doubt, but also in our houses and huts and bothies. They'll have to forage, but they'd never ride up here, so far from their ships. They're intent on reaching York as fast as they can. Speed and surprise. They're powerful weapons."

"Right!" Wilf told the weary villagers. "Duty. Do what you have to do. Feed your animals; feed yourselves; help each other; rest and pray to God."

"Amen," said Father Huw, and he drew the sign of the cross over his flock.

Maybe having to do everything, and do it together, will help us all, thought Kata. Being sorry for ourselves won't get us anywhere, and neither will dreading what the Vikings may be doing in Riccall.

Time limped past.

Down in York, it was exactly the opposite.

Time hurtled. It careered.

The whole population – almost ten thousand people – seemed to be out on the streets, jamming the passageways, jostling and crowding in the open spaces.

Everyone knew the time of waiting, the uncertainty and suspense, were almost over. And they were relieved about that, even though they'd heard that the Vikings were massing just downriver.

Not only was there a sense of dread but a new, fierce energy and almost a kind of gaiety.

As soon as he rode into the city that evening, after meeting Arni and Bard, Tor had to work his way round a packed crowd sharing scurrilous songs and jokes about the Vikings. When he reached the courtyard by the earl's residence, it was no less crowded than when he and Kata had stabled her pony there yesterday.

It seemed more like three weeks.

Tor elbowed his way through the crowd so as to get as close to the entrance of the hall as he could.

"What's happened?" he asked an old man with only one eye. "What's happening?"

Before the man could reply, a guard came out of Earl Morcar's hall, with two heralds who blew their bugles, and the crowd quietened down.

"This message from Godwinson, our king," the guard called out. "This message from Godwinson."

Slowly, everyone fell silent – everyone except the babies wailing in their mothers' arms, inconsolable at being jolted and squeezed.

"Earl Morcar and Earl Edwin sent the king a message four days ago," the guard called out, "telling him that Viking warships had entered the Humber."

"Speak up!" shouted one man.

"Shut up!" ten voices replied.

"This is King Godwinson's reply," the guard said. "'My September army is stationed here on the south coast of England, keeping watch in case Duke William, William the Bastard, sets sail from Normandy. The winds have been against him for ten days. But here and now, my poor people, your need is more pressing. Your need is now. I've ordered my leaders to strike camp early tomorrow morning, and we'll ride and march north to York.

"'We'll spread the word – we'll rally more men on our way. But my people, my dear people, there's no chance of our reaching York for ten days, or longer. It's almost three hundred miles from here to York, and my men can only march twenty miles a day. Have your people downriver delay the Vikings in every way they can. Let heaven come to help us with storms and floods. Dear men and women of York, you must defend and save yourselves as best you can.'"

It's a mercy Godwinson's army is so far away, thought Tor. For my father to engage with the earls, and maybe fight them, that's one thing, but I don't think he'd want to fight against the earls and Godwinson at the same time.

When their English scouts came in late that night with news that the Viking fleet had already arrived at Riccall, and started to disembark, Earl Morcar and Earl Edwin were left with no time to delay.

They summoned to the hall their small team of councillors, as well as those headmen from the hundreds who had already arrived in York with their villagers, armed not with swords and shields but pikes and pitchforks, and sickles and wooden clubs.

Earl Morcar stood up. "We're all agreed, aren't we? We're all agreed that we simply can't defend our city walls."

Many men shook their heads, and most bowed them. There was no one in the hall who spoke against him.

"Of course we can't," Earl Morcar continued. "They're not even in good repair. So we've no choice. We'll have to take the fight to the field. But that's not the worst thing."

"Exactly," said Earl Edwin. "Have you all heard how Hardrada – when he was young – how he massacred all the women and babies and little children in one city?"

"He's a cruel man," said his brother. "If we fight in the

field, at least we'll avoid a massacre."

"But he's only just arrived in Riccall," Earl Edwin added. "Our best weapon is time. Time and surprise."

"Right again!" said Earl Morcar. "The quicker we are, the less ready he'll be to counter us. Does anyone here disagree?"

There was silence in the hall.

Outside in the courtyard, a few of the crowd had started to disperse. But most had remained, anxious to hear what the earls and headmen had decided, and Tor was one of them.

It wasn't long before word got out, as words do, that the earls and their army would be riding out of the city at ten o'clock in the morning.

"We'll follow the course of the river as far as Fulford Gate," one guard told Tor. "Latecomers must meet us there."

Tor chewed on his pony's leading rein, uncertain what to do.

Shall I try to tell my father? Should I? What difference will it make? He's not spoiling for a fight, and I'm sure he'll offer terms to the earls first.

"God is on our side!" yelled the man with one eye. "Our side!"

And very soon dozens and dozens of men were waving and shouting. "Our side! God's on our side! We'll hammer the Vikings."

CHAPTER 22

It was already very late when Tor approached *Mævill*, and he saw that Matason's wife, Safæ, and the two slaves, Razon and Mundir, were all on their knees in prayer, leaning forward so that their foreheads were touching the deck.

Tor paused at the bottom of the gangway and inclined his own head. First, he thought of how often Odin and Thor had fought the giants and defeated them, and then he began to think about God the Father and about Jesus.

I don't know anything about the Moorish gods, he thought. Does it really matter which gods you worship? What was it that old prophet said? *For everything there is a season – a time for war, and a time for peace.*

"Inshallah," Matason's wife called out, and then she and Razon and Mundir voiced in unison, "*Inshallah.*"

Tor strode up the gangway, springy beneath his feet.

"Are you eager to leave then?" Tor asked Safæ with a smile.

"What?" asked Safæ.

"Ready to sail."

"What?" said Safæ. "And break the blockade? Break the warning that boy gave us?"

"As soon as they see you," Tor replied, "the Viking ships will make way for you! The Red Sea will part for you!"

Safæ gave Tor a knowing smile, but then she pursed her lips. "You," she said. "We have this saying. Don't tease a woman unless you are her husband."

Tor grinned. "Where is he, anyhow? Is he going to obey orders? Obey that little boy?"

"Talking to the other skipper again," Safæ replied. "Who was he, anyhow? That boy. Do you know?"

"No idea," said Tor.

"I think you do."

"Nothing to do with me."

"Where's Kata then?" Safæ asked him.

"Up in Poorhoe, I hope. Out of harm's way."

"That's good. I like her. I like her very much. It was the same for her mother and me. Kata told me she was a slave and mistress to a Swedish skipper, Red Ottar, on his trader."

Tor nodded. "I'm hoping Matason will let me stay on board tonight – me and Skopti. It's not safe in the city. Feverish."

"I'm sure he will," said Safæ. "He barks a lot but he's a good man."

Then she sat down, crossed her legs, and settled again to her mending, while under the bows, Razon and Mundir lay down on two mats, and drowsed.

Mævill swayed gently, and when Tor woke at sunrise, he thought at once of his meeting with Arni and Bard.

Did they meet my father, and did they tell him about meeting me? Yes, they must have done. I've been wondering half the night what he'll make of that – because I made it sound as if I'd talked to him too.

And I've been wondering what he'll decide to do. What if he decides to work his way right round Earl Morcar's and Earl Edwin's army instead of meeting them at Fulford Gate? What if he outflanks them, and marches straight here? Everyone in York would be defenceless.

Whatever happens – I mean, whatever I decide to do – I must be here this evening in case my father decides not to parley with the earls but to advance on the city.

The gates of York. That's what I promised. Otherwise, I will have betrayed him.

Tor jumped to his feet and threw off his thick, woollen sea coat. He stretched, he yawned. And then he realized that Matason had already left his boat again.

He must have jumped down onto the towpath without my even hearing him, Tor thought. He's double my age but as fit as I am. He's probably gone off to check for news about when the earls' men set off for Fulford Gate, and how many there were, and maybe talk to the other skipper.

Oh, Kata! Kata! How can I honour you both – you and my father? I don't even know how far it is up to Poorhoe. I know I promised you I'd come, but I can't be in two places at the same time.

Tor stared at the water kicking and swirling and splashing around two big rocks upstream from *Mævill*.

If we hadn't met... I mean, if I didn't really care about you... But I do. I do! How is it you and Hilda and Oswald came down to Bullfrog's watermill at exactly the time when I was there too?

Tor took a deep breath. I know... It's fate. I know.

Then he cupped his ears and listened intently. He could hear the distant strains of monks chanting.

And then he heard – or did he simply imagine that he could hear – the far-off, repeated war cry of the English. "Oot! Oot! Oot!"

Around him the early morning air was gentle and mild, and little birds flitted upstream, downstream, and kept criss-crossing the river.

It's too soon to go into the town, he thought. There can't be any news yet. But this afternoon...

Tor yawned. And his thoughts turned to his mother, Solveig, and her great journey – when she was only fourteen, a year younger than he was.

She told me how a Swedish skipper took her aboard as one of his crew... What was the name of his boat? Something stirred in Tor's brain. What was it? Something that Safæ had said – about her own life being so similar to Kata's mother. How Kata's mother had been a slave on a Swedish ship...

No! It can't have been. How can it?

I was only half listening.

Tor began to tremble. His heart began to race.

All morning Tor was edgy and indecisive, walking from bow to stern and from bulwark to bulwark, slapping Skopti on his rump and feeding him fresh grass, and asking Safæ when she thought Matason would be back, and examining the stores in the hold and sometimes rearranging them.

Nine thousand of us, thought Tor. Nine thousand Vikings. That's far, far more than the earls can possibly recruit from all the hundreds around York, and anyhow most of them will be fighting with pickaxes and knives and won't even be wearing armour.

Nine thousand. It will be a bloodbath.

"What's wrong with you?" Safæ asked him. "What's the saying? You're getting under my feet."

Tor didn't answer her. I feel so … so tired, he thought. Tired of waiting, tired of half-truths and pretending, tired of… I feel so weary. He sighed, he yawned, and at the end of the morning, he threw himself back onto his pallet, and actually dozed through the afternoon.

Perched on *Mævill*'s masthead, a raven barked and cackled and roused Tor.

It's so quiet, he thought. So very quiet. What's happened?

It's like our graveyard when the fjord's lying low. And that little church in Riccall where Kata showed me the fish, and the tops of our heads just touched. And like that chapel at Trondheim where Saint Olaf sleeps, and I cut his little toenail. Like any place, I suppose, where the quick and the dead rub shoulders.

But it won't be so quiet inside the city.

Tor shouted down to Safæ that he was going ashore, and then ran along the gang plank and headed for Coppergate. First, he heard loud sobbing inside one building, and then a furious argument inside another, and wailing in the distance.

Without knowing what's happened, he thought, without knowing a thing, I feel I already know everything. Which side am I on? I'm not on any side. I just wish none of this was happening.

At the entrance to the market, Tor saw a young woman kneeling on the ground, crouching over a sack. No! Not a sack. It was a body.

The woman was shuddering but not making a sound.

Tor broke his step. He looked down at her. He didn't know what to do.

Then the woman levered herself up, and Tor looked at the body. And at the sticky blood that had stained the ground.

"I couldn't..." she said in a low voice, "I couldn't stop him." And then she shook terribly. "He ... said ... said he'd got to go."

"Go to Fulford Gate?"

The young woman nodded. "Like all his friends. Everyone. To fight against Harald." She caught her breath and sobbed. "We married last month."

Tor screwed up his eyes.

"Didn't you then?" the young woman asked him. "Did you go?"

Tor shrugged.

"Why not?" she demanded. "Tostig was there. Earl Tostig!

Killing his own countrymen." The young woman bent again over the body of her husband and enfolded him in her arms. "And almost ... almost he came back, all the way from Fulford. But look at the stabs... Here in his stomach."

Tor stared down at the poor young woman. She's the same age as Kata, he thought. Much the same.

"May God..." he began, rather shakily. "Well, may God give us all peace."

"Why not you?" she persisted. "Why didn't you go and fight?"

But Tor didn't answer. What could he say?

I can't tell her, he thought. I can't say I'm not on either side, but just obeying orders. She wouldn't understand.

As Tor walked into the market and the late September sun began to settle into a swaddling of pink-and-purple clouds, he fell into step with a host of other people heading in the same direction, not to put up their stalls, not to compete with each other's street cries, but to tell each other what they had heard about the bloody battle at Fulford, and to ask each other what would happen next.

The longer he wandered around, and the more snatches of conversation he heard, the more Tor realized that everyone had a different tale to tell.

One said there were ten times as many Vikings as English; one that Earl Tostig had only reached Fulford Gate well after the battle was under way. One said yes, but ... one said no.

In fact, the only thing everyone agreed on was that all the September rain had turned the battle site into a terrible, sucking gluey marsh, and Hardrada had tricked the English into breaking their shield wall and wading into it, and that once they were in, they couldn't get out, and couldn't even find a secure footing so as to wield their battleaxes.

"Dozens were drowned," one woman told Tor.

"Dozens!" repeated an old man. "*Hundreds* more like, lying side by side in the squelch. So many that the Vikings could walk across the marsh, standing on their bodies."

As he listened, Tor felt more and more oppressed. His head began to ache. His whole body ached. While he'd long known there was bound to be fighting between the Vikings and English, only now did he understand that in York, where they had lived side by side for so many years, and traded, and relied on each other, and even married each other, the battle was a terrible disaster, and both sides were the losers.

CHAPTER 23

Earl Morcar and his elder brother, Earl Edwin, had a great deal to fear but very little to discuss. They had left almost as many men cut down and drowned in the flooded water meadows as there were survivors, and early that evening, as soon as they had ridden back to York, they summoned their councillors.

"If it wasn't plain before, it's plain enough now," Earl Morcar told them. "Without help from Godwinson and his army, we'll be overwhelmed. We've already lost upward of six hundred men. And our scouts say Hardrada's army numbers nine thousand, and that's without counting Earl Tostig's supporters. Eleven thousand then! If we fight them inside the city, our men will be put to the sword, our women raped and massacred."

"To think Earl Tostig fought alongside Hardrada..." Earl Morcar raised his voice. "How could he?" he shouted.

"How could he and his followers betray us, his own countrymen?"

"He's a traitor," growled Earl Edwin. "A murderer. No fate is bad enough for him."

"It seems to me," said Earl Morcar – his voice was flat, his expression stony – "we have only one choice. One choice. Whether to live or die. There's no dishonour in choosing to live."

Earl Edwin nodded. "A losing side can't make conditions."

"We must submit," said Earl Morcar.

There was no argument in the hall. None.

So the earls instructed five of Earl Morcar's most experienced councillors to find King Harald and inform him, and him alone, that Earl Morcar was offering to submit York and all its citizens to him.

The councillors left very early the next morning, following the same way along the river that the English army had taken only the previous day. And when they reached Fulford Gate, they were horrified to see not only hundreds of floating corpses but seven Vikings splashing around, wrenching helmets and gauntlets off some of the dead men and prising their weapons out of their hands. One of them stared at the councillors, and then he brandished a shining sword, and laughed in their faces.

"Carrion thieves!" one councillor shouted.

And another, "Worse than the beasts of battle."

And another, "Devil's brood!"

The councillors learned from a couple of wounded Viking stragglers, lying beside the river path, that King Harald had returned to his ship at Riccall immediately after the battle.

And that was where they found him, standing on the deck in the company of his two skalds.

At once all the five councillors lowered themselves onto their old knees. "Earl Morcar greets you," their leader said. "He offers to submit to you. He offers to submit the city of York and all its citizens."

Hardrada swallowed. He sucked his mouth dry. "And so say all of you?"

The other four councillors nodded.

"Well, go on! Let's hear it from each of you."

Still on their knees, each man repeated Earl Morcar's words.

Harald Hardrada took a deep breath, and then he padded slowly round the deck. Several times he paused and tugged his grizzled beard.

"Right! Up on your feet!" he told the councillors. "Greet Earl Morcar for me and tell him that I'll send him my reply tomorrow. Tomorrow at midday."

The Englishmen inclined their heads and turned away. They stepped from ship to ship back to the riverbank and their horses, relieved to have accomplished their mission.

"So many miles," their leader said. "So few words."

"He never spoke of the battle," said another man as they rode along the path to the watermill.

"Nor of Tostig," added a third. "Not once."

"Harald must despise him," their leader replied. "A turncoat. A traitor. But he needs him, and I'm sure, quite sure, that he's offered Tostig great rewards."

CHAPTER 24

That evening, three separate warehouses in Coppergate were torched and burned to the ground, with all their stock inside them – silks and spices, beaver pelts and the fur of black foxes, sealskins, whale blubber. Each of them belonged to a Norwegian who was married to an English woman.

A thick, stinking shawl of smoke lay over the market.

And it wasn't long before grief and tears turned to fury and more reprisals.

Gangs of men, young and not so young, charged from street to street; steel blades flashed; women and children hid behind doors.

That night, Tor slept safe on *Mævill*, and when he ventured back into the market to check what was going on, he ran into Arni and Bard. They were both flushed and dishevelled.

"Are you all right?" asked Tor. "What's happened?"

Arni looked at Bard; Bard looked at the ground.

"Well?" Tor demanded.

"See that church up there? An old woman came out and started screaming."

"Screaming!" Bard repeated.

"About what would happen to all the Norwegians. Hellfire and flames and torture," said Arni. He looked at Bard again.

Tor screwed up his face. "You killed her."

"Her own words did," Arni muttered.

Bard nodded.

"You've been drinking," said Tor.

The two scouts shrugged.

"And you … you think that's what he wants, do you?"

"Who?"

"My father."

"She insulted us," said Bard. "She threatened us. Anyhow, who are you to tell us what to do?"

"The king's son," said Tor.

"His bastard, more like," Arni said. "His half-son."

Tor clenched both fists. "Drinking," he said loudly. "Drinking and killing. Killing a woman."

Arni took a stride towards Tor and butted his forehead. "You buzzard! You two-faced liar! You lied to us when we met you and you told us you'd been with the king all day. He said he hadn't seen a wart or whisker of you."

"So what were you doing?" Bard demanded.

"Yes," said Arni. "Why were you riding back into York?"

"How can we make peace? How can we," Tor pleaded, "when even we are at each other's throats?"

Arni and Bard advanced on Tor. Arni took his left arm, Bard his right.

"You're right," said Arni. "It makes no sense at all. None!"

"What?" demanded Tor, jerking himself free.

"This bad blood."

"We're on the same side, aren't we," said Bard.

"We can sort it out," Arni added. "This evening."

"What do you mean?"

"We've talked to your skipper. The skipper of your trader."

"Matason, isn't it?"

"We explained."

"Explained what?" said Tor.

"We need somewhere to bunk down. Somewhere safe. York's a hellhole."

"You mean you told him who you are?"

"Friends of yours."

At this moment, the three of them were interrupted by a terrible howl from up near the church.

Arni and Bard grabbed each other.

"Come on!" Arni urged him.

"Scarper!" said Bard.

And the two of them ran helter-skelter out of Coppergate.

Later that morning a pair of Viking messengers galloped from Riccall to York, and they reached Earl Morcar's hall at midday.

Hardrada's reply was not a long one.

"King Harald accepts your submission. He will meet you

outside the city walls at noon tomorrow to discuss terms and reach an agreement."

And that was that!

So while Godwinson was still many miles away down south, delayed by arguments with local headmen about how many men they could release from their farming duties, frustrated by a shortage of horses that could be recruited at such short notice, and drenched by thrashing rain… Harald Hardrada set off for York early the next morning with his entire army, now somewhat rested after the fight at Fulford. Bringing Earl Tostig and his Englishmen with him, Harald reached the gates of York on Saturday at noon.

Hardrada offered a hand of peace to Earl Morcar, and likewise to Earl Edwin, and at once told them he had no wish to punish them or the citizens of York.

Then King Harald beckoned Earl Tostig, and the earl stepped forward and offered his right hand as well. But neither Earl Morcar nor Earl Edwin would shake it. They refused even to look at him.

Tostig, they thought. He's behind all this, Behind Harald… His one aim is to win back his earldom. Our Northumbria.

"I ask for no payment," Hardrada said. "You're not buying me off. I'm your rightful king. I suggest that we exchange hostages as a sign of our good faith, a sign of trust. One hundred and fifty of ours, one hundred and fifty of yours, including the sons of your foremost men."

Earl Morcar pursed his lips and rubbed them. He looked at Earl Edwin, who was standing beside him.

"Not only this," Hardrada went on. "My interests are

your interests. Godwinson's no lasting friend of yours and no friend of mine. He wants to be recognized as absolute king of this whole country... We could combine our armies. We could march south and fight him. Three armies in one."

And then you'll depose me, thought Earl Morcar, and restore this kingdom to Tostig. Over my dead body you will! He gritted his teeth.

Tostig's thin lips curled. He narrowed his foxy eyes. He said not a word.

"Yes, I understand," said the young earl quite calmly. "Well, we won't agree on each and every issue today. I accept your suggestion — to exchange hostages. When and where shall we meet?"

Hardrada nodded. "Two days... Is two days long enough for you to round up your hostages, and prepare lodgings for mine? Monday at noon."

"Agreed," said Earl Morcar. "Where?"

"Halfway," replied Hardrada. "Halfway between York and Riccall." Then he turned to Tostig. "You know the lie of the land better than I do."

"Every inch of it," Earl Tostig said. "In my blood and in my bones."

"Where then?" demanded Hardrada.

"The bridge at Stamford."

There was a great press of people around the leaders, but King Harald quickly spotted his son among them. As soon as he and the two earls had concluded their discussion, and again exchanged the hand of peace, he shouldered his guards aside and advanced on him. "Where in the nine worlds have you been?"

Harald Hardrada glared down at Tor, and his left eyebrow kept jumping as if it had a life of its own.

"Where have I been?" Tor repeated. "Everywhere! All over the city. In villages and hundreds. At that watermill at Riccall and—"

"All right! All right!" said the king, swatting away his son's recital.

"Watching … listening … asking … scouting. Your last words to me at Scarborough were that you'd see me at the gates of York. Yes, and here I am."

"You scoundrel!"

"No, Father. I'm not."

The king stepped right up to his son, and he growled, "From what I've heard, you've been spying on me, not on the English."

"No, I can explain."

"Explain what?" demanded Hardrada. "I don't want explanations. I want information."

"Yes, Father."

"Don't you understand? You're my own son. I long to be able to trust you and rely on you. Why, I really don't know. Or rather," he said, "I do know. I know very well."

"Sire?"

"Because of your mother. The way she saved me, and nursed me, and… That's why I give you such slack."

Harald Hardrada clamped his hands on Tor's shoulders, and Tor flinched.

"Sore?"

"I had a fall, sire."

"A bad omen," said the king, and for a moment Tor leant his forehead against his father's left shoulder.

"Now, Tor! I want you to stay here in York with Arni and Bard, and I want you three to keep a close watch, hour by hour, on Earl Morcar's movements. Him and Earl Edwin. How many messengers he sends out to recruit hostages from the hundreds. What he's saying to his foremost men – and what they'll be telling their sons. And listen, too, to what the people are saying. Listen very carefully."

Tor nodded. "Yes, sire."

"Keep your eyes about you. Keep your ears to the ground. And come with Earl Morcar to the bridge at Stamford."

"Yes, Father. I will. I promise I will. Trust me."

"What you find out will help me to make choices and save Viking lives. Monday at noon."

Tor ran all the way back to *Mævill*. He had to go back now; he needed to get his pony. He knew his fate was closing in on him – and that he'd have to keep in step with his father now – but he was determined to ride up to Poorhoe first, and see Kata.

There was no one aboard apart from Safæ.

"What's the hurry?" she asked.

Tor untied his pony.

"Half-afraid," said Safæ. "You are, aren't you? You're out of breath."

Tor shook his head.

"Being brave doesn't mean you're not afraid," Safæ told him. "Half-afraid. It means going ahead anyhow."

That's true, thought Tor.

"Your friends, Matason said they asked to sleep aboard last night. The same as you. But they didn't show up."

Tor shrugged. "They're not my friends."

"What about you, Tor? Are you staying tonight?"

Tor tossed back his long, fair hair. He hesitated.

"I don't ... I don't know," he stammered. "Well, it depends…"

On Kata, Tor thought.

Matason's wife tilted her head a little on one side. She smiled. "We have a saying. *A young woman in love is an angel living on earth.*"

Then Tor untied his pony.

CHAPTER 25

Heading up to Poorhoe, Tor rode through a wood and past a shepherd's stone bothy, then up and over a grassy rise, along an old black hedge, and at once he saw men and women and children scattered in front of him, all waving their arms and stamping and making a din. Tor pulled up.

It's not like lashing waves or whip cracks, thought Tor. And not like the hammering in a forge. What is it? A mixture of hooting and clapping and the rattling and the clattering of metal bowls and pans and screeching. What is it?

It's a hubbub. A pandemonium. It's unlike anything I've ever heard before. Wolf-whistling! Loud-mouthed cowbells!

What are those people doing? he wondered. Are there ghosts up here? Are they chasing away dead spirits?

But then he recognized the young man nearest to him – making straight for him, banging two large stones together.

"You again!" he said.

It was Oswald.

"What are you doing?" exclaimed Tor. "What's going on?"

Oswald jeered. "You don't know?"

Tor shrugged.

"Tanging."

"What's that?"

"What you can hear." Oswald waved his arms, and he clashed his two stones.

"What for?" asked Tor.

"To settle the bees, of course. They're swarming, and we found a hive up here. Exactly what we need, seeing as we couldn't bring ours up from Riccall."

"And this, this uproar – it settles them?"

"You heard what I said."

"How?"

"How do you think? It stops them from flying away."

Tor shook his head. "Who says?" he demanded. And then, "Do you know what bees do if it gets dark while they're still on the wing?"

Oswald shrugged.

"They lie upright to protect their wings from rain and dew."

"Rubbish!"

"Tor," said a deep voice right behind him.

"Father Huw!" said Tor. He inclined his head. "You're not..."

"Tanging," said Father Huw. "Not this late in the year. Better say a few prayers. Bees are good Christians!"

Tor laughed and dismounted.

"Think about it. They give us sweetness for our food and

drink. And with their wax, they give us candles to lighten the dark. There must be bees in Norway, aren't there? Anyhow, if you happen to be looking for Kata, she's over there with the headman and Hilda. Mattie and Ellette, too. Not that Wilf will welcome you."

But Kata had already seen Tor and was hurrying towards him.

How handsome she is, he thought. Striding. Her sweet chestnut hair all higgledy-piggledy, with a life of its own. How bold. And she always looks as if she's about to laugh.

Kata raised both arms towards Tor, but then she thought better of it and lowered them, and lowered her eyes too.

"I was sure you'd come," she said in a low voice. "But sometimes I wasn't."

"Me too," said Tor. "And I know I'm later than I said."

"Two days," said Kata. "Two whole days... Wilf is telling each of us our duties. Me and Hilda and Mattie and Ellette. Come!"

So Tor walked his pony alongside Kata, and Wilf shook his head and clicked his tongue. "I didn't want you to come," he said, "but I can't say I'm surprised. And seeing as you're here... Well, we've got everything in the world to do if we're going to survive until the spring."

Tor nodded seriously.

"We must be quite, quite sure we've got food to last through the winter. Oswald and Snell and Rinan and all the men must start hunting, and I've just been telling these young women to pick all the fruit they can find and carry. There are not so many fruit trees up here, but it's a good harvest. Apples, red plums, damsons, pears."

"Quince, too," said Ellette.

"What bothers me most…" said Wilf, and then he broke off. "You're listening, are you, Kata?"

"I am!" Kata protested.

"We can't get at any of the grain stored in our barn, so we just won't have enough."

"I remember the year," Mattie told them, "when our wheat was flattened by hail. And the barley wasn't much better."

"I remember that," said Wilf.

"And what we did … we mixed in all sorts with the grain. Nettles and roots, even grass."

"And acorns," Wilf added.

"Acorns, yes, and bean pods. And we shared the beech mast with our pigs."

"First things first," Wilf told them. "Fruit picking, and drying, boiling, all that. And hunting."

"I could scout around," said Tor, "in case any villages round about have grain to spare."

Wilf looked at Tor under his shaggy eyebrows. "You're staying then?" he asked.

"No," said Tor. "I mean, well, I'll come back."

"It's true," Wilf told him. "We do need help. First to get dry roofs over our heads. And Oswald… I'm sure he could do with a hand later digging more latrine pits." He gave Tor a knowing smile.

So, for the remainder of the morning, Kata and Tor worked side by side, replacing the slates on the roof of Kendra's stone hut while she hobbled around, gathering moss and stuffing it into all the cracks in her walls.

The wise woman looked up at Kata's and Tor's handiwork. "Light's a better friend than dark," she observed, "but not when it comes through the roof."

Kata smiled. "You and your sayings."

"I know another one," said Tor. "I think I do. A Swedish one."

"My mother wouldn't have liked it," exclaimed Kata. "She didn't like anything Swedish."

Kendra tapped her stick on the stony ground. "Well, go on."

"Um… Some afternoons find out … yes, that's it. Some afternoons find out what the mornings never suspected."

"Very true," agreed Kendra. "Things don't always turn out as we plan or want them to."

"They do change for the better sometimes," Kata said. "Like the weather."

For his part, Tor realized that while the villagers were working so hard, he would have very little chance of spending time alone with Kata.

"You know I'm ready to help," he told her. "But can't we have time for ourselves? Everyone will understand."

Kata sniffed. "Yes," she said. "Especially Oswald! On our way up here, nothing was too much trouble for him. And he even offered me a swig of sweet apple juice."

Tor shook his head. "I've got an idea."

"What?"

"There's a stone hut. Over there, down at the foot of the long slope."

Kata nodded.

"I saw it on the way up." Tor hesitated. "It's deserted.

Well, I could pretend I was leaving. I could ride out of this village, away down the long slope, and through that wood and…"

"You mean…"

"I mean, you could come down when it's getting dark, and no one would notice. I've got something to tell you."

CHAPTER 26

A little while before the light began to fail, Tor left Poorhoe. He cantered down the long slope, and through the beechwood, and at least a mile beyond it. Then he pulled up and began to talk to Skopti, and to rub his neck, and thank him for being such a trusty companion.

The pillow clouds drifted. They looked as though even they weren't sure which way they were meant to be blowing. It's like this in the fjord sometimes, Tor thought. Summer's ending.

He was filled with a certain calm – the calm of certainty.

Kata, he thought. Kata. I'm meeting you, you and no one else.

After all this harum-scarum, this toing and froing and having to pretend to you, and everyone in Riccall, and Bullfrog, and Matason, and even my own father, I was starting to believe in my own stories.

Tor slid off his pony and tightened his sea coat around his waist. He picked a pink-petalled daisy, inspected it, twirled it between his fingertips, and tucked it behind his left ear. He stared at the huge, orange moon just surfacing in the east.

I'm always hurrying, he thought. But there's time now. Time... Kata. He smiled, and dropped the reins, and stretched his strong arms. There'll be plenty of time to do everything my father wants me to do after I get back to York.

Inside the hut, Kata held her breath and listened to the sounds of the pony whinnying and Tor dismounting and tying him up to the big stone with an iron ring embedded in it.

Only then did she show herself, smiling and stooping slightly under the lintel.

She had washed herself with water from the stream that ran, swishing and gurgling, right past the hut, and she had swept back the cascade of her chestnut hair, and tied it with a twist of honeysuckle.

Then she laughed, and he laughed. And it was just as Safæ said. *A young woman in love is an angel living on earth.*

Tor reached out, and Kata stepped straight into his arms.

There was a low stone table inside the hut – a single rough grey slab that must once have taken at least two people to carry it. And on the table Kata had laid out three platters. One with pieces of raw carrot and radish and a lump of soft cheese, one with walnuts and hazelnuts, and one with fruit – pears and plums and blackberries.

Tor shook his head and smiled.

"Kata!" he said. "What a feast! It's a banquet!"

"Oh!" Kata exclaimed. "The way you lay words... Well, lay words at the table of what you say."

Tor raised both eyebrows. "I'd never have thought of saying anything as lovely as that!" he said.

Then Kata bent down and picked up a little candle from under the table. "Real beeswax," she told Tor proudly. "Its scent will be stronger than the sour smells, and the light will push – push the gloom into the webby corners."

As soon as Kata had lit the wick with a spark from her little tinder box, she reached under the table again and fetched out two jugs and then two wooden mugs.

"You brought all this down here?"

"Ale, this one," Kata told him. "And this one, mead."

She was shining.

Then each of them sat cross-legged at the table – Kata facing the door, Tor to her left.

Kata joined her hands in prayer. "Earth, oh Earth, our Mother Earth!" she said. "Feed us now, feed us always."

"What a feast," Tor said again. "Thank you, Kata. From my heart! That's what me and my mother say."

Kata laughed, and she pulled Tor towards her, and nuzzled him, and then she poured ale into each wooden mug.

"Alone," said Tor. "You. Me. At last."

Kata caught her breath, and very slightly she shook her head.

Tor put both hands over his heart. "Words," he said. "Words."

"What?"

"They're so strange. We need them but sometimes, well, they're not enough."

Kata nodded.

Tor gave a deep sigh. "You've heard about Fulford?"

Kata screwed up her eyes. "Horrible!"

"Who told you?"

"A messenger. Riding round from village to village."

"Yes," said Tor. "Horrible!" He shook his head. "And then it spilled over."

"What do you mean?"

"People in York arguing, attacking each other. Killing each other."

Kata's eyes widened.

"What I've heard is your earl has agreed to submit," Tor told her. "He'll submit the city and everyone in it. He and Hardrada are meeting on Monday to hammer it all out."

"I thought," said Kata, "well, I hoped Godwinson – he's our own king – I hoped he would come and help Earl Morcar."

"He's too far away," said Tor. "Much too far."

"So…" Kata began. But then she hesitated. She didn't know exactly how to ask.

"Yes," said Tor. "Me and you."

Kata lowered her head.

Tor reached out and wound a wisp of Kata's hair round his little finger.

"You said you'd got something to tell me."

"I did!" said Tor. "And ask you."

"What?"

Tor chewed a piece of carrot and took a swig of ale. He grabbed Kata's left hand and squeezed it and the blackberry inside it.

"Watch out!" she exclaimed.

Tor laughed. "Well, I don't know…"

"What?"

"… how to begin." He smoothed the silken hair growing around his chin. "What was your mother's name?"

"Edith," said Kata with a smile. "So?"

"My mother … my mother is Solveig."

Kata's dark eyes were wide and shining. "Solveig," she said softly.

Tor nodded. "And she told me the mistress of Red Ottar, the Swedish skipper on her trading boat, was a pretty English girl…"

Now Kata was shaking. Shaking and laughing and sobbing, all at the same time.

Then Kata and Tor pieced together the story, the long journeys each of them had heard from their mothers, and each half knew. And how Tor had pieced it together because of what Kata had told Safæ.

How Solveig and Edith became friends as they sailed south to Kiev, and south again from Kiev down a large river called the Dnieper. How they had to portage their boat round seven roaring cataracts, only for mounted horsemen called the Pechenegs to shoot volleys of arrows at them. And how Red Ottar choked and died with one arrow sticking out his mouth.

Yes, and how Kata's mother, Edith, realized that she was going to be burned alive on Red Ottar's funeral pyre because she was his slave. And how Solveig argued with the crew, and said it could not possibly be right to put anyone to death who had done no wrong, let alone a young girl with Red Ottar's own baby leaping in her womb…

Kata and Tor stared at each other, flushed and excited and triumphant.

They both laughed; they both wept. Then Kata grasped both of Tor's hands, and began to tell him even more.

"My mother said she loved your mother so much they could have been sisters. She said it was a miracle she ever got back to Riccall from thousands of miles away… She lost her baby with Red Ottar, but when she reached home, she got pregnant again and that was with me."

"So who was your father?"

Kata shrugged.

"I think this is what happened. When my mother came home, everyone in Riccall was astonished, and everyone was so happy. And Wilf – he became our headman after the Swedes killed my mother's husband – he hired music-makers from York or somewhere to come and play and sing and rejoice… What I've heard is that everyone drank too much ale and mead, even my mother. And then she took one of the music-makers back to her hut…"

Kata winced.

Tor gave a deep sigh.

"And later that night the music-makers rode away, and no one knew where they had gone, or their names, or anything."

"And one of them was your father?"

Kata sniffed. "I think so. Yes."

"Oh, Kata!"

"How can it be…?"

"What?" asked Tor.

"How can it be that without our even knowing … without *our even knowing*, our mothers met, so long ago, so far away… And now we've met? Well, and everything?"

Tor shook his head. "Not … by chance," he said slowly.

"How can it be? What does it mean?"

Tor smiled. "It's fate."

"What does it mean, though?"

"What I think…" Tor began. "Well, I think such a wonder tells us that we were meant to meet."

CHAPTER 27

Up in Poorhoe, a bell began to ring.

"What's that?" asked Tor. "I mean, what's it for?"

"Compline," Kata told him. "The last of our prayers. You know, David says, 'Seven times a day do I praise thee.'"

Tor shook his head.

"'Lighten our darkness, we beg you, O Lord, and save us from all the perils and dark dangers of this night.' We don't actually meet to pray, though, because most of us are already half-asleep."

Kata and Tor listened for a while to the reassuring tolling of the bell. Then they stood up, stepped out under the moon – high in the sky already, no longer orange but buttercup – and they dovetailed their fingers.

They drew close. Mouth to mouth, lips to lips, they gently kissed.

"Kata!" whispered Tor.

"What?"

Tor didn't reply at once. He looked up at the moon.

"What?"

"There's something else."

"What do you mean?"

"Well! I'm not what you think."

"What do you mean?"

"Not who I said I was."

Kata frowned.

"I'm not a fisherman. At least, I don't fish for fish."

"Snell and Rinan told me that," Kata replied, smiling and shaking her head.

"What?"

"'He's no fisherman. He don't know nothing about fish!'"

Tor didn't reply.

"So?"

"I'm a scout," said Tor. "A scout for King Harald."

Kata put her firm hands on his shoulders and, in the moonlight, she stared into his eyes.

"Not a very good one," Tor added, and Kata burst out laughing.

"Tor! You think I didn't suspect?"

Tor shrugged.

"You could have told me before. Couldn't you?" She stared at him. "Does it make things different?"

"Different?"

"You and me?"

Tor shook his head.

"But it makes all the difference in the world to tell you," he said. "To tell you the truth."

Kata gathered Tor to her. "Oh, Tor!" she murmured. "Tor! Who are you then? And when, and where from…? Tell me everything. Everything! What you said about your mother and mine – that's true, isn't it? Oh, please – that's true?"

Tor nodded. "It is. All of it."

"Is it true what you told me about Earl Morcar offering to submit, and him and Hardrada meeting on Monday to exchange hostages?"

"It is."

"And you really think everything will be settled soon, and there'll be peace?"

"Yes, Kata. Yes. On Monday."

"And before then, what are you going to do? What do you have to do?"

"What I'm meant to be doing."

"What?"

"Scouting. Gathering information."

"For Harald?"

"At first light, I must ride down to York. To York, and then Riccall, maybe. To try to find my father."

"Your father?"

Tor nodded.

"You never told me," Kata said. "He's here too?"

Tor sighed and shook his head.

"And then on Monday – after the exchange of hostages?" Kata asked eagerly.

"I'll come back. Back to you. At once!"

In the dark, Kata was laughing and weeping, both.

"Come now," Tor said gently. "Come!"

Then Kata took Tor's warm hand and led him into the stone hut.

Wilf's cockerel woke Kata and Tor. Its crowing and the day's first sunlight leaking into the hut around the ill-fitting door.

Kata drew Tor to her – his shoulders, his hips, his thighs, his toes. And for a minute, they lay there unmoving, silent, two-in-one.

Then Tor sprang up, flexed his shoulders, and shouted, "Kata! Kata!" And then, "Oh! Kata!"

Kata lay and watched him swig the lees of the ale left in his tumbler. He flicked the last drops at her and chewed a mouthful of cheese. Then he ran naked to the stream. She heard him splash himself all over.

Kata wrapped herself in Tor's filthy old sea coat, took a deep, deep breath and slowly let it all out again.

Oh! I could stay here all day, she thought. Just laze and dawdle and drowse, like we do at Yuletide.

When Tor stepped back into the hut, he announced, "A gift for you."

Kata smiled.

"It's not exactly a lover's gift – a breastpin, I mean, or a girdle, or a comb or anything like that. But it's the most precious thing I've got."

Tor knelt down beside Kata and began to feel along the hem of his coat.

"What are you doing?" asked Kata, still smiling.

Then Tor found what he was looking for, and he ripped the hem with his teeth. The little walrus ivory box fell out.

Carefully, he opened the box and showed it to Kata.

Kata wrinkled her nose. "A nail," she said. "A toenail. What is it?"

"A toenail, yes. Saint Olaf's toenail. I cut it myself."

"Who said you could?"

"My father. Oh, I'll explain. It's a holy relic, Kata. For as long as you keep it safe, you'll be safe yourself. It'll keep you safe from breath to breath, and hour to hour, until I come back."

Then he wrapped his arms around Kata, and her eyes widened and filled with tears.

Gently, Tor wiped them with the back of his right hand. "*Skira*," he said.

"What?"

"*Skira*. Baptise. Your tears, they wash us."

"*Skira*," repeated Kata. "Like the sharp-soft sounds metal and stalks make when they meet during scything. Scrape and scour and skirmish too ... and Scarborough. They sound the same."

"There are lots of Norwegian words that begin like that," said Tor, and he fingered his beard. "*Skegg*," he said.

"Silk," said Kata, laughing. "Silken."

"Yes and no," said Tor, slowly stroking his chin. "*Skegg* means beard. And *skinn*?"

"Skin."

"Yes!" Tor held up his sea coat. "*Skyrta*," he said.

"*Skyrta*," Kata repeated.

"Coat," Tor told her. "And *skina*," he asked, smiling and running his fingers through Kata's hair.

Kata pulled Tor to her. "Skiss," she exclaimed. And she kissed him. His forehead. His cheeks. His lips. "Skisses, skisses, skisses, hundreds of them!"

She broke into a torrent of hot tears.

Tor held her tight. "Kata, Kata!" he comforted her.

Kata shook her head and stared at Tor. Then she picked up something from the rug at their feet.

"What's this?" she asked.

Tor smiled. "Oh! A daisy. Pink-petalled. I picked it for you on the way here. I meant to give it to you."

Then Kata sobbed again.

Tor began to wrap his sea coat around his shoulders, but he thought better of it and took it off again. "Keep it safe," he told Kata. He drew her to him, and kissed her gently, gently and lovingly, and then very firmly.

So they stepped out of the little stone hut, and Tor mounted his pony. They lowered their eyes, then slowly their eyes met.

Tor cantered away.

CHAPTER 28

Tor strode up the narrow gangway, and Skopti followed him.

"Well, well!" Matason growled. "Safæ! Look who's here." He confronted Tor, and barked, "Where the devil have you been?"

Tor was startled. He blinked, but then he smiled and opened his arms. "Up there!" he said. "As high as the clouds."

Safæ looked at Tor under her long eyelashes.

"Your friends – Arni and Bard – they're scouts," said Matason. "And so are you. They said so. I told that girl not to trust you."

Tor stuck out his chin and took a step towards the skipper. "You'd better trust this then," he said.

"What?"

"Harald Hardrada requires you and the other skipper to house as many of our Norwegian hostages as you can take aboard. And you're to feed them. Whatever they want."

"What!"

"The ones we're exchanging for Earl Morcar's men. They'll be safe here. So that's … what? Almost seventy-five men on each boat."

Matason rounded on Safæ. "Hear that?" He swore under his breath. "Who says so?"

"Who do you think?" Tor retorted. "Those are your orders, and you're to relay them to the other skipper. And my orders," Tor told him, "are to ride straight back to Riccall."

I wish I didn't have to lie, thought Tor, and put words and orders into my father's mouth. What's more, he's told me to stay in York. But I want him to see I'm thinking for him and can make a difference.

Matason stalked down to the stern, swearing again.

Safæ smiled at Tor. "It was … what you hoped?"

"Oh yes!" said Tor, and he pressed his right hand to his heart. "Yes."

"May Allah go with you always," she said, and she fingered the little silver box fastened to the belt around her waist. Quickly she opened it and pressed something into Tor's right palm.

"For Kata," she murmured.

"What's going on?" Matason demanded.

"You won't have to house the hostages for long," Tor called out. "King Harald believes we'll all soon be allies, and march side by side south to fight Godwinson."

Matason sniffed, and Tor led his pony back down the gangway.

He remounted and opened his right hand. In his palm, clear as finest honey, nestled a tiny, rounded, glowing drop of amber.

So when can we be together? Me and Kata, thought Tor. Not tomorrow. There's the march to Stamford Bridge, and exchanging hostages, and even if that's straightforward, it's going to be a very long day.

Tuesday morning. Or afternoon. The afternoon anyway.

Halfway to Riccall, just beyond the water meadows at Fulford, Skopti grew reluctant to canter, and before they reached the Viking fleet, the pony was limping.

"Poor creature!" said Tor. "I'm the king's scout, and you've been this scout's best friend."

Tor led his pony along the riverbank until they reached the king's ship. And there he stood, marvelling at her.

Between clouds, the late afternoon sunlight burnished the gilded weathervane at the top of the mast a full forty feet above Tor's head. It singled out the gold stripes on the tiller and lit up the sixteen overlapping shields hanging from the bows to the stern.

When a light north wind brushed the sky clean of clouds, the ship's dragon figurehead gleamed, all the strakes shone, and the whole ship looked as if she were made of dancing flames.

All this, thought Tor, all this, and then there's everything I can't see – the lashings of deer sinews below the waterline, and the plugs of animal wool, and the stays, the sockets…

Suddenly, Tor realized he was thinking not only about

Hardrada's ship but about Kata. Kata, so curved, so light, so beautiful … and he laughed.

Not tomorrow, I know. But the next day.

He gazed at the ship again.

"Tor!" boomed Harald Hardrada. "Tor!"

Tor raised both his hands.

The king was standing alone beside the mast, and his crew were all sitting on the far bank of the river, eating and drinking.

"Come over here! Come on!"

So Tor stepped lightly from boat to boat, and over a shield into Hardrada's ship, and he was smiling.

"I told you to stay in York. In York with Arni and Bard. That's what I said."

Tor looked his father in the eye.

"I told you to check how many messengers Earl Morcar's sending out, and what he's saying to his leaders, and what the townspeople are saying."

"I know. Yes."

"I told you to come to Stamford Bridge with Earl Morcar."

Tor nodded.

The king grunted.

"I should never have brought you with me. I told you I was depending on you."

"Father…"

"What now?"

"I wanted you to know."

"Know what?"

"I wanted to tell you that I've ordered Matason – he's the skipper of one of the two trading boats – I've ordered

199

him to stand ready to receive our hostages, the men we're exchanging for Earl Morcar's men."

"What?" boomed the king.

"And I've told him to instruct the skipper of the other boat to stand ready as well."

"On whose authority?" Harald demanded.

"Well, sire. Well, mine and yours. Actually, I collared a boy in Coppergate a few days ago and bribed him to come to Matason's boat with a message that the skipper was not to weigh anchor and leave York."

"You mean you told this Matason that those were my orders? Is that what you did?" The king stared down at his youngest son, and slowly shook his head, and then suddenly burst out laughing. "God in heaven!"

"This way," Tor explained, "our men should be safe. No one in the town will be able to harm them. And today I've instructed Matason to lay on food and drink, and tell the other skipper to do the same."

"I see!" said his father. "So what you've done is put words and orders into the king's mouth."

Tor nodded.

"Men have lost their heads for less," the king said in a stony voice.

Then Harald Hardrada stepped forward and swept up his son in an almighty bear hug.

When Tor had regained his breath, he said, "I wanted you to know I've been thinking for you. I wanted you to be proud of me. And there's another thing, sire, another reason why I'm here. Tomorrow you're riding to Stamford."

"I was aware of that," said his father in a dry voice.

"I began this journey with you, when you allowed me to cut Saint Olaf's nail... I want to see Earl Morcar submit. I want to be standing beside you. I'm your son."

"Listen to me!" Hardrada said. "At Stamford, it could be dangerous. Earl Morcar and Earl Tostig hate each other. Tostig spent half the summer with me, and he persuaded me to attack England because he wants his earldom back. He wants Northumbria back. But his people don't want him. They threw him out. Because he was greedy, greedy and murderous. Old dogs never change their spots... But now Tostig's telling me that many villagers from all over Yorkshire are already coming to join us, and they're ready to march south with us against Godwinson." Harald paused. He sighed. "Are they, really? And anyhow, what good would they be against Godwinson's swords and axes with their sickles and scythes? What if Tostig double crosses me?"

Hardrada cleared his throat and spat into the river. "I really don't know what to think." He waved downstream. "Tostig's just behind us now. He had only twelve ships when he met me at the mouth of the Tyne, so how come he has seventy now?" The king clicked his tongue and sighed. "All right!" he said loudly. "All right, Tor. You're coming with me."

Tor locked his hands in front of his chest and shook them. "Thank you, sire! Thank you!"

"Armour? Have you got armour?"

"No, sire."

"Go and see Skuli, my armourer."

"Sk–Sk–Skuli."

"Why are you laughing?"

Tor shook his head. "For happiness!" he said. "For joy, Father."

"Our trumpets will sound twice at dawn, and after that Tostig and his followers will join us. Be ready then."

Tor nodded.

"You can sleep on this ship. But I must talk now with Young Olaf. Who's to come to Stamford? Who's to stay and guard our ships? Three hundred ships, Tor!"

"And who will serve as hostages?" Tor added eagerly.

King Harald pursed his lips. "Thank you," he said.

"Have you already chosen them?"

"It's called forethought. It's called leadership."

Tor nodded.

"But leaders must rely on their scouts," King Harald said, narrowing his eyes at his son. "They're our eyes, our ears."

"Yes, Father."

"King Harold Godwinson! Poor man! He's been waiting for weeks in Kent for the Normans to attack. But the same wind that blew us down to the Humber is holding up Duke William in Normandy. So now ... now Godwinson's caught in a pair of pincers."

Hardrada shook his grizzled head. "Well, not even a king can be in two places at the same time."

CHAPTER 29

Each and every thing was singing.

The north-west wind began to bluster, the thorn trees hissed, and the long grasses swayed, pods rattled their black seeds, little shoals of veined sycamore wings shuffled and scraped where the ground was hard and dusty.

Singing and shining. The old black hedge was jewelled with scarlet rose hips, and the darker red berries of the hawthorn, the flashing silver ovals of the whitebeam's leaves. The glistening papulae of the sweet-sour blackberries.

Kata hurried up to Poorhoe, carrying what she could. I'll come down and collect the platters and everything after dark, she thought.

As soon as she got back to her hut, she stuffed a lump of soft cheese into her mouth, and then sucked a juicy pear. I'm hungry, really hungry, she thought. I could eat a whole rabbit.

But it's so sore, my mouth. My lips… She laughed out loud, and then she squeezed her eyelids tight and wrapped her arms fiercely around herself, and she crooned.

When Kata stepped out of her hut, she saw a huge bundle of grass weaving its way on two legs across the yard, or what used to be the yard, crusted and uneven now, thick with weeds as well as many shrubs.

It was Puttnam, the reed-cutter, and he was heading straight towards her. In fact, he would have collided with her if she hadn't stepped nimbly out of his way.

Puttnam dropped his huge bundle.

"Jesus go with you," said Kata.

"And you, Kata," said Puttnam, wiping his brow. "Thought I'd get started on your roof."

"Why mine?" asked Kata. "What about Wilf's, and Father Huw's?"

Puttnam gave Kata a sort of sideways smile.

"What are you smiling about?"

"Just came into my mind."

"It did, did it?" Kata couldn't stop herself from laughing.

"Well, you lost your lovely mother this summer, didn't you? And I dare say you'll be our headwoman, next after Wilf. You know… This and that."

"And what?"

Puttnam winked at her. "Somewhere nice and warm like, when the cold days come on."

Kata narrowed her eyes at the reed-cutter. "You! You … spy!" she exclaimed.

Puttnam shrugged. "I saw you, I did. Carrying stuff back from the bothy."

"You didn't!"

"Mum's the word," said the reed-cutter. "Mind you, these grasses! Unless I lay them thick as thick, they'll let through as much rain as they keep out."

"The roof's ruined," Kata said.

"No good trying to patch it up. It's sour and grey and mossy. I'll take it all off."

Kata hurried across the yard to fetch Puttnam's ladder, and when she had marched it back, Puttnam told her, "It's fifty years, more maybe, since these cottages were thatched. My dad, he helped with some of them."

"Your dad?"

"When he was a boy. They brought the reeds up from Riccall and Fulford. But because of the plague, everyone had to move away. The whole hamlet. But not before seventeen died."

"No!"

"It's like waves," said Puttnam.

"What is?"

"Plague … and then those Swedes attacking Riccall…"

"They took my mother away," Kata said. "And killed my mother's husband."

"My father as well," said Puttnam in a low voice. "Yes, the Swedes, and then bloody Tostig stealing more and more from us – more money, more wheat, more cattle – leaving us skint. And now it's the Vikings."

Kata listened, and tenderly laid a hand on the reed-cutter's right arm.

"What lasts..." said Puttnam. "What lasts is what I like. Upstanding stone churches, well built, and ... cherished. Is that the word?"

"I think so."

"And trees that have lived so long our grandparents and great-grandparents courted beneath them. Things that stay the same. That's what I want. That and the river, slow breathing. In and out, in and out."

"I heard a song about that," Kata told him. "Well, about how years wreck everything. My mother sang it to me."

"Go on then," said Puttnam.

"Roofs have caved in," Kata began. "Yes, that's it."

"Roofs have caved in, towers collapsed,
barred gates are broken, hoar frost clings to mortar,
houses are seeping, tottering and falling,
undermined by age..."

Puttnam sighed. "Time," he said. "That's a thing you can't do anything about. But caring for what your family helped to make, you can do that."

"Come on then," said Kata. "Let's get started."

Hot work it was, and Puttnam and Kata were grateful for the cooling north-west wind as they ripped the rotten old thatch from the roof of Kata's hut.

"I can't explain it," the reed-cutter went on, "Father Huw could. It's sort of sacred... Things going on. It has to do with families, and remembering. Things go on, and even though they change, they're still the same. Because of them, well, we're rooted."

"That's why old poems matter too," Kata added. "There's a riddle about reeds."

"What?"

"How they grow, and make music, and make words..."

"Tell me later," Puttnam panted. "I can't work and listen at the same time. We haven't got any reeds anyhow. Only this grass."

"Look!" exclaimed Kata.

Puttnam looked up. He saw that a man on a grey mare had just appeared from behind the black hedge and was cantering into the yard. Kata jumped down from the roof onto the pile of old thatch, and then held the ladder so Puttnam could climb down. Like everyone else, they converged on the horseman.

When the man dismounted, Kata saw that he was wearing a large silver bracelet on his right wrist.

"Earl Tostig's messenger!" he announced grandly.

Wilf stepped in front of the other villagers. "Tostig's not an earl," he retorted. "Not any more he isn't."

The horseman scowled. "Like that, is it? Haven't you heard, then, about Harald Hardrada? King Harald of Norway?"

"Haven't I heard?" Wilf repeated scornfully. "Haven't we all heard?" The headman shook his right fist. "And haven't you heard how we've all had to leave Riccall?"

Several of the villagers shouted insults at the horseman.

Kata gave a loud sigh. "At least let him speak," she sang out.

"Hardrada and Earl Tostig are joining forces," the messenger said. "They'll ride south together against Tostig's brother, King Godwinson. And they require Morcar and his men to ride with them."

Wilf gritted his teeth.

"You know the rule. Each village, each hamlet is required to provide one fit man from each family to join the army."

"What?" exclaimed Wilf. "Join Tostig's army?"

"And Hardrada's army," said the messenger. "To reclaim our own kingdom. To fight against Harold Godwinson. Everyone's enlisting – men from York, the Vale of Pickering, the villages along the Ouse and Derwent."

"No!" said Wilf. "I'm not having a single man from Riccall join your ... mob! Harold Godwinson is our rightful king. Harold Godwinson!"

The remainder of what the headman had to say was drowned by the cheering of all the villagers.

Wilf held up his hands. "I know what's going on," he called out. "The next thing... The next thing Hardrada will do is reappoint Tostig. He'll make Tostig his liegeman and Earl of Northumbria again."

On all sides, the messenger was assailed by scorn and insults. Pursing his mouth and shaking his head, he remounted and slowly wheeled away.

Oswald had crept up behind Kata, and Eager stood right behind him.

"Norwegians!" said Oswald in a loud voice.

Kata jumped and turned round to face them.

"They're not trustworthy."

Kata immediately rounded on him. "Says who?" she demanded.

"Well, are they?" Oswald bellowed. "What about Tor? Who do you think he is?"

More caring than you, thought Kata. Much more. And he's not against us. He's not on either side.

Many of the villagers heard him and shook their heads, and several felt sorry for Kata.

"Come on," said Wilf. "Back to work. Come on, Eager."

Then all the villagers dispersed, some of them alarmed at what Tostig's messenger had told them, and some troubled by Oswald's anger. Puttnam and Kata climbed back onto her roof.

"What a fine singing voice you've got," he said, and he smiled at her.

As soon as Father Huw had rung the midday bell, Kata thanked the reed-cutter for his help and ran down to the stone hut. She was upset at Oswald's angry words in front of all the villagers. But when she threw herself down on her pallet, she at once began to think, to think and smile, smile and half dream of the last time she was there.

Within a few minutes she fell fast asleep.

Kata woke smiling, and then she burst out laughing. Laughing at the way in which Tor had winked at her when they first met at Bullfrog's mill, winked so fast that neither Hilda nor Oswald noticed.

He's so quick, she thought. So clever in his mind and speedy with his tongue. Sometimes he thinks he can do things faster than he really can, but that's because he's so alive, he's a risk-taker.

I'm not like that at all. I know Wilf says I'm a leader, and people trust me, but why does Tor ... I mean, what is it about me?

He relies on himself, and he's so strong, and he told me he thought I was the girl he'd been waiting for all his life, and he meant to find out...

Oh, Tor! I think I am. I believe I am.

I'd do anything for you. I'd go anywhere.

Kata jumped up. She skipped out to the little stream and splashed her face and arms. Then she dived back into the hut and crammed her mouth with plums and blackberries and cheese left over from the night before and, after that, she chewed on one carrot after another.

Sitting on Tor's sea coat and leaning against the wall, she began to think of each and everything that had happened, minute by minute, after Tor had ridden up here the evening before – how they had talked about his mother, Solveig, and how they had found out that she knew Kata's mother, Edith, because their fate had been interlocked, and how Solveig had actually saved her mother from being burned to death on a funeral pyre...

But now! Kata asked herself. What are we to do now? Tor and me. What is our fate?

We can't stay in this village or in Riccall, she thought. Not with Oswald... Can we both go to York? But what if Hardrada wants to take Tor south with him?

Kata splayed her fingers and ran them through her hair so that it just danced on her shoulders.

Anyhow, she thought, I think Tor wants to go home. Back to his farm. Solveig's forty-six, so she must need help.

I'd like Solveig, I know I would. She could tell me lots more about my mother. What she was like when she was young. And whether I look like she did. And what happened after Red Ottar was killed. Where ... and when...

One thought after another chased through Kata's mind. The days and decisions to come. Here and now!

Where is he? In Riccall?

Why does time sometimes pass so quickly, sometimes so slowly?

Has he been thinking about ... well ... about us? And everything? And coming back? And this stone hut?

Tomorrow, he said he'd be back. No, not tomorrow because of the meeting at Stamford, and it being such a long day.

Tuesday, yes, that's what he said. Tuesday morning.

CHAPTER 30

Harald Hardrada burst out laughing when he saw Tor clanking and stumping across the deck towards him.

"Absurd!" he bellowed.

"I'll get used to it. Skuli says I will."

"It's far too large for you."

"It's all he's got left."

The king took a couple of steps backwards and appraised his son. "You look as if you've never worn armour before."

"I haven't," said Tor, and his voice was muffled because his helmet had tilted right forward, and the nose piece covered his mouth.

"What?" said the king.

"Skuli says he can stuff in more padding."

Hardrada chuckled, and he stepped forward and raised Tor's helmet. "There!" he exclaimed. "Look around you. Christ and Njǫrd are on our side."

"Sire?"

"The weather! Not a cloud in the sky."

Tor nodded.

"You're in luck. I've just been talking again to Young Olaf and my leaders, and we all agree there's no need for our men to wear full armour. Whether we're riding or marching, we'll all get much too hot if we're wearing helmets and breastplates. It's a long stretch from here to Stamford, and all the way back again."

"Escorting the English hostages?"

"Exactly!"

"They won't be wearing armour, will they?" asked Tor.

"Most certainly not. And without a single weapon between them. When we get back, we'll confine them on three of our warships here."

"What about you, Father?"

"What do you mean?"

"Will you not wear armour?"

"You're a crafty one, aren't you?" Hardrada said. "I never go anywhere without my suit of armour. Emma, she's called. Yes, Emma and my banner, Land Ravager. It's always better to be wary."

"Is it true," Tor asked, "that the Empress of Byzantium gave you Land Ravager? When you served in her army?"

"Zoe," affirmed Hardrada in his deep voice. "Yes, she did." And he raised his head and stared away into another time, another place. "Yes. 'This banner,' the empress told me, 'was made by witches fifteen generations ago. Prayers are sewn into it; spells are stitched into it. For as long as it flies before you, you'll never come to harm.'"

Harald Hardrada looked down at Tor.

"And so it has been," he said quietly. "Yes… Your mother was there, you know."

Tor shook his head and smiled.

"What a fine, brave young woman."

"She told me the banner is coloured copper and saffron," Tor said. "And woven with little crimson dots and crosses."

The king nodded and sighed. Then he clicked his tongue. "But here and now," he said. "That's what counts. What always counts. Have you eaten?"

"Sire?"

"Have you eaten? This morning?"

Tor shook his head.

"Get on with it!" his father told him. "Here and now! The second trumpets are about to blow. Go and find some food."

"Eystein, your marshall – he says that he's staying here with Young Olaf to guard your ships. My Skopti has gone lame, but he says I can borrow his fine horse, and…"

But then the trumpets did blow, and a long procession of English men from Tostig's ships started to make their way along the river path. Those men who had them took off their helmets and breastplates and piled them in the foremost Viking boats moored alongside the riverbank, glad to follow Hardrada's advice and Earl Tostig's instructions on such a hot morning.

And so, leaving behind them one third of their army – three thousand men – to guard their ships under the leadership of Young Olaf and Eystein Orri, King Harald and his leaders, and Earl Tostig, set off in high spirits for Stamford, and Tor rode with them.

"That's a good, strong horse you have under you," Tostig said to Tor.

"It belongs to Eystein," Tor replied. "Eystein Orri."

"My marshall," Hardrada told Tostig. "A fine young man. He's just asked me whether I'll allow him to marry my little Maria. Your half-sister, Tor."

Tor thought he'd rarely heard his father sound so full of feeling.

"For the first time in my life," Harald told his son, "I understand how Yaroslav felt – Yaroslav of Kiev – when I told him I wanted to marry his daughter."

"How old was she?" asked Tostig.

"Twelve."

Tor drew in his breath.

"Just twelve, yes. He made me wait, of course. Yes, and what with his two elder daughters marrying the King of France and the King of Hungary, and all the discussions and arrangements, he had his hands full, all right."

Harald Hardrada fell silent. And then he sighed.

"Maria, she's so frail. She gets sick so often. I hope she and her mother are being well looked after in Orkney."

"They'll be thinking about you, and talking about you," Tor said. "And Young Olaf as well."

"And even about you," said Hardrada. "They both care for you. I can't think why."

"And I care for them," Tor replied. "I always have."

What with being fitted out in armour, and talking about Emma and Land Ravager, and grabbing something to eat and drink, and setting off with Hardrada and Earl Tostig at the head of the Viking army, Tor had scarcely had a moment since waking to wonder about Kata – what she was doing, what she was thinking and feeling – let alone to relive the precious hours they had spent together in the stone hut.

But now, well on the way to Stamford, and surrounded by his father's and Tostig's army, now he couldn't stop thinking about her.

The way she's so fast on her feet, not like the girls at home who always look at the path in front of them. And the way she laughs and opens her arms, and smiles at me with her shining eyes. They're hazel with green flecks. You can see how all the other villagers look up to her. That's why Wilf took her with him to York. He trusts her.

And the way she gets so flushed… Her face… Well, her whole body! I think she's as strong-willed as I am, but that's all right. She needs to be. It's the same with girls at home. When they marry, they have to run the whole farm as well as bear children.

I like how curious she is. How eager. She always wants to ask questions, but she doesn't mind not knowing everything. I mean, how could she, living in Riccall all her life? And without a father. It's different for me. I know most of my days and months are up at the farm, but because of my father, and sometimes attending his court…

I'd trust her with my life.

I would.

Tor shivered. He'd never thought anything like that before.

I've found my way back to my father. He accepts me and he's honouring me by having me ride with him and Earl Tostig. I know that.

And I managed not to have to fight at Fulford. I didn't want to. I know I've done other things I didn't want to do, like stealing Skopti on my way south. But I was on my own, I had to. And I lied to Matason and wish I hadn't.

Tor's thoughts kept going back to Kata. I can't imagine my life without her. I want to take her back to my farm. I want my mother to meet her. Edith's daughter!

Just imagine! Edith's daughter!

All the things I'll show her. Norway will be a whole new world to her. All the words, and the sagas, and dark days and laughter that we'll share. All our loving. All the days of our lives…

Suddenly Tor remembered his dream. He and Kata were in Riccall, and Kata was standing on one side of the river, Tor on the other. They kept calling out to each other, and they were tying paddles and oars together, so they could walk on water and meet in the middle. And then—

"Tor!" exclaimed his father. "Did you hear that?"

"What, sire?"

"What do you think? Is Tostig right? Do the Vikings and the English really have more in common than divides us?"

"Er…"

"Your head was in the clouds," Tostig said. "It was, wasn't it? Young men have better things to think about."

"Actually," Tor replied, "I have been thinking about that. I have."

Tor was saved from saying anything more because Earl

Tostig raised his right hand and pointed at the long rise in front of them. Unlike the land behind them – well wooded with old oaks and ashes – it was open, and empty apart from a few grazing cattle, and a ruined bothy.

"A mile," said Tostig. "No more than a mile, and you'll see Stamford. Down in the valley in front of us."

"Right!" growled Hardrada.

"It's nothing much to speak of. Only a little village. But because of the bridge across the river, it's a crossing place."

"A meeting place," Hardrada added. "Well, let's hope Morcar's here already. With his hostages."

But what Harald Hardrada saw as he reached the top of the rise, followed by his army, some on horseback, most on foot, was not what he hoped for or expected at all.

On the gentle hillside across the river, he saw a cloud of dust raised by the hooves of horses. And below that he saw gleaming shields, and shining coats of mail.

At once the king halted.

"Who are they?" he demanded. "Tostig?"

Earl Tostig narrowed his eyes. He shook his head. "I can't be sure… More recruits, are they, coming in to join us from the vales and dales?"

"Or?" demanded Hardrada fiercely.

Tostig didn't reply.

"Wearing helmets, wearing coats of mail," the king snarled. "I think not."

Tostig drew in his breath. "You're right," he said. "Who the devil are they?"

"Right!" announced Hardrada. "We'll halt here. Six thousand men! Your men as well! Six … thousand … Vikings!

We're not going one step further until we find out, but we're not turning back."

The king sat high on his black horse and stared at the army advancing down the long sweep of green land on the other side of the river, spreading out as they did so.

He tugged at his beard and never took his eyes off them, not for one moment.

Neither did Tor.

The longer they looked, and the closer the army came, the more it swelled, until there were ranks of men everywhere, to the left and to the right and in front of them, everywhere down to the bank of the river.

And in the bright, late morning sunlight, their glittering mail coats and shields and swords and spears shone and sparkled like a field of broken ice.

CHAPTER 31

"Godwinson," barked Hardrada. **"It's Godwinson. Of course it is. Who else could it be?"**

Tor caught his breath and he flinched.

Earl Tostig knew better than to say anything.

Beneath his thick grey beard, Harald bared his teeth.

"How can it possibly be? He can't have covered such a distance so quickly. His mounted men, maybe, but not his men on foot. He can't have done."

"Sire…" Tostig began, but Hardrada ignored him.

"I should have posted guards between Stamford and York. Of course I should. I've never made … never, never made such a mistake."

"We're in danger, sire," Tostig warned him.

"Do you think I can't see that?" snapped Harald. "Very great danger. I've been tricked."

"We must turn back."

The old king widened his eyes, and he glared at Tostig.

"We're only half-armed," Tostig said. "These leather jerkins, they can't withstand English arrows. As for their swords, their spears…"

Hardrada took a deep breath.

"We must!" Tostig urged him. "If we get back to our ships, and our weapons and armour, we can fight this army and beat them."

"We can, can we?" Hardrada said. He pushed out his lower lip and threw back his head. "No!" he shouted. "I'll send three men back on our fastest horses…"

"Eystein's horse here," said Tor.

"… and they can alert Young Olaf and everyone. As soon as they know what's happened, they'll all ride here as fast as the wind."

"I'm going," Tor said. "On Eystein's horse."

"No!" growled his father. "I want you here at my right hand."

"Sire…" Tor began.

The king turned to Tostig. "Believe me, even if the battle starts before all our men get here, the English will have a bitter time of it."

"Sire…" Tor tried again.

Hardrada shook his head. "Beside me, Tor. I want you beside me. At my right hand. I fought at Stiklestad when I was fifteen."

Tor quaked. He pulled his shoulders forward.

"Well, Harald…" Tostig began. He gave a deep sigh.

"I've not come all the way from Norway to give ground to Englishmen," Hardrada retorted.

Then the king himself rapidly rounded up three men to gallop back to Riccall, and he ordered his flag officer Fridrek to raise his banner, Land Ravager.

At once the north-west wind pounced on it. The thick copper-and-saffron silk snapped so loudly that even the gods in Asgard could hear it. Harald's magnificent black horse, Midnight, heard it too, and it unnerved him. He neighed and backed away. Then he reared up and the king was only just able to stay in the saddle.

"Whoa!" he shouted. "Midnight. Whoa!"

But Midnight snorted and kicked up his back legs and, although Hardrada grabbed hold of the white blaze on his nose with both hands, Midnight threw him.

At once Tor dismounted, but before he or any of the king's companions could help him, Hardrada levered himself onto his knees and then scrambled to his feet and shouted, "That fall – it's good fortune. You know the saying."

No! Not everyone did. Several older warriors lowered their eyes.

And what Hardrada quietly said to his son was, "That fall! It was farewell to fortune."

On the other side of the river, King Godwinson was watching.

"Who's that?" he asked. "The man whose horse threw him. Wearing a blue tunic and a shining steel helmet."

"Harald Hardrada," one of his companions told him.

"Was it, indeed!" Godwinson exclaimed. "What a giant he is. Well, let's hope he's run out of luck."

"Now then," announced Hardrada. "We must shape ourselves up. Step by step. The more time we take, the less time it will be until Eystein and all the others get here."

First of all the king drew up his whole army and Tostig's followers – almost seven thousand men – as a single very long thin line, just five men deep, along the grassy ridge above the village. Then he ordered the two wings of the line to bend back and a little sideways and keep on stepping back until the whole army formed an enormous circular shield wall.

Once all the Vikings and Tostig's men had shuffled backwards and sideways and forwards again to Hardrada's satisfaction, and he'd ridden right round the circle to inspect them, here and there drawing up to encourage them, he instructed a few dozen men to break rank to allow him and Tor and Tostig and their chosen guards to position themselves inside the shield wall.

"Right!" he said. "Now, I want my archers with me here inside the wall, surrounding me."

"Look, sire!" exclaimed Tor.

Twenty English horsemen were cantering over the wooden bridge across the River Derwent, and they and all their horses were wearing coats of mail.

Hardrada watched as they rode right up the slope to the Viking shield wall. Then one man shouted, "Tostig! Earl Tostig! Is he here with this army?"

Inside the circle, Tostig walked his horse a few steps forward. "He is!"

Then a second Englishman at once called out, "Your brother, the king, sends you his greetings. He offers you the hand of peace. If you'll join forces with him now, he'll give you the whole of Northumbria. One third of his entire kingdom."

Earl Tostig sat very still in his saddle. He glared at the man, and loudly sucked his cheeks. Tor watched wide-eyed as he walked his horse round and round, before pulling up in front of the English horsemen again.

"He will, will he?" Tostig called out. "So he's singing a different tune now. If he'd offered me anything of the kind last winter, many dead men would still be alive, and our country would be at peace. So if I accept my brother's offer, what will he offer Hardrada?"

He can't, thought Tor. Tostig can't desert my father now. Can he?

"The king," replied the second rider, "is prepared to grant Hardrada seven feet of English ground. Seven feet, or as much taller as he may be than normal men."

Earl Tostig took a deep breath. "No!" he shouted, and then he and his horse barged through the shield wall and right up to the rider.

"No," he said again. "Go now and tell your leader to make ready to fight. I'll never have the Vikings say that Earl Tostig abandoned Hardrada." Tostig looked back over his left shoulder at King Harald and Tor. "We share one purpose and one fate. We'll conquer England or we'll die."

At once the twenty horsemen wheeled away and cantered down to the bridge and crossed it to their own lines, and Tostig walked his horse back inside the shield wall again.

"Who was that man?" Hardrada demanded. "The second one? The man who spoke so clearly and firmly?"

Tostig looked him in the eye. "That," he said slowly, "was Godwinson."

"Godwinson!" exclaimed Hardrada. "Your brother! You should have told me." The king growled. "He'd never have escaped with his life."

"It's true, sire," said Tostig. "My brother was taking a huge risk, and he might have lost his life. But he wanted me to see him and hear him – my own brother. He wanted me to hear what he was offering me. My life. The Earldom of Northumbria."

So brave, thought Tor, and he shook his head. He was risking his life.

"If I'd told you who he was," Tostig said, "I would have been his murderer. I'd rather he killed me than I him."

Hardrada grimaced and he slowly nodded. Then he turned to the men inside the shield wall. "Well," he called out, "what a little man that Godwinson is. But he stood proudly in his stirrups."

Then the King of Norway bowed his head, and Tor could hear he was chanting something to himself.

After a short while Hardrada gazed up at his companions, and he intoned:

*"Now we advance
into battle
without armour,
and fight against blue blades.
Our helmets may glitter
but our coats of mail
and all our armour
are back at the ships."*

The king sucked his cheeks and said in some disgust, "That was really a very poor verse." He tugged his grey beard. "I'll make another one."

Tor looked up again, and he could see that not only crows but ravens and buzzards and sea eagles were gathering overhead. They knew the signs of battle, and they were screaming for blood.

"Right!" said Hardrada, and he drew himself up to his full height in his saddle.

Tor gazed up at him. What is he planning? he thought. What is he feeling?

His father answered him.

*"You must never bend your knee
or crouch behind your shield
to save yourself from the weapon storm.
That's what my mother once told me.
Always hold your head high in battle
when swords swing and shatter
the skulls of fated Norsemen."*

In the front line of the Norwegian army, there were more than a dozen berserks – the specially picked warriors wearing bearskins who worked themselves into such frenzy in battle that even their companions sometimes became terrified of them.

Tor saw them crouching and heard them chanting, louder and louder. Then they all sprang into the air, and howled, and whirled round and round.

And there was another warrior no less fearsome than the

berserks. He was actually only forefinger span shorter than Harald Hardrada, and as broad-chested as two men. He said he was the son of two trolls and came from the frozen north.

Hardrada allowed this warrior to range wherever he chose – the king had seen him cut down Swedes in battle like field corn, and half-believed he had magical powers.

"Me," the troll-man bawled, "I'd never go anywhere without wearing my helmet and mail coat. I'm no fool." He rounded on his companions. "I'll lead the way. None of those English will be crossing that bridge."

The troll-man strode down the rise to the riverbank and up onto the wooden bridge. He raised his double-headed battleaxe, and he opened his throat, and roared.

Then two Englishmen stepped side by side up onto the bridge. The Viking swung his axe, and with a single stroke, he beheaded them both.

Tor couldn't believe his eyes.

Up near the top of the rise, the berserks howled like werewolves.

Tor watched as three more Englishmen advanced on the troll-man…

And then four…

The troll-man cut them down and hacked them into pieces. He tossed their heads and arms and legs and torsos into the swift river, and the water swept them away.

Then Tor and the Vikings saw that three Englishmen were picking their way down to the riverbank, only a little upstream from the bridge. One was carrying a pike and the other two were rolling a beer barrel down into the water. With the help of his companions, the man with the pike tucked himself into it.

Seeing this, dozens of Vikings ran down the grass bank, shouting warnings to the troll-man, but he didn't hear them.

Rocking from side to side, the barrel bobbed down the river, and when it was right under the bridge, the Englishman grabbed one of the wooden stanchions. Peering up at the underside of the bridge, he made out a small gap where the bridge's planking had come slightly apart, and that was exactly where the troll-man was standing.

Tor cried out when he saw what was going to happen.

The Englishman drove his pike up through the opening. He thrust it between the Norwegian's legs, right up through his groin into his vitals.

The troll-man screamed. He collapsed.

So at last Godwinson's men began to cross the bridge. They streamed across, they came at a run, but not before they had already lost thirty-nine warriors.

Yes, thirty-nine companions, cut down by the Norwegian troll-man.

Tor could scarcely believe what he had just seen. He was appalled. And he was scared.

The English massed up in the green water meadow beside the river – hundreds of men. Thousands. And on either side of them, there were curtains of weeping willows.

Slowly they started to walk up the rise towards Hardrada's great circle of Vikings.

Tor bared his teeth.

Godwinson's men cheered.

Hardrada's men jeered.

There was shouting on earth.

CHAPTER 32

Kata realized she was shivering.

She felt so fearful.

She walked out under the afternoon sun, with Tor's sea coat around her shoulders, and shook herself like a terrier.

Why is it like this? she wondered.

But no sooner had she asked herself than she could hear Father Huw consoling her, "*Lacrimæ rerum*, Kata, *lacrimæ rerum*. The tears of things... Be hopeful. Always be hopeful."

She sat down beside the spring, weeping softly.

Is this what it's like, loving? Does it have to be?

Why am I so afraid?

She stared down at her white knuckles and realized how tightly she was gripping the little bone box with Saint Olaf's toenail inside it, and sobbed out loud.

I wish he'd taken it with him, she thought. He's the one

who could be in danger, when they exchange hostages.

Where are you now, my Tor?

Somehow, all the women in the village divined Kata's need.

Young and old, alone and in pairs, they made their way down to the little stone hut that Kata had adopted.

Not only Hilda and her mother, Mattie, for once not arguing with each other but walking quietly side by side, and the wise woman Kendra hobbling along on her stick, but Ellette with her little daughter, Bliss, and May, Borden's sister, who had walked up to Poorhoe to visit her brother, and Orva too, who had fished every bend in the Ouse with Snell and Rinan but was stranded now up at Poorhoe, like a fish out of water.

They sat down quietly around Kata. And for some while none of them said anything. There was no need.

Then an arrowhead of pink-footed geese flew in from the north, honking and heading for the marshland around Riccall and Fulbourn. Staring up at them, Kendra observed, "When they come back from the north, and settle in for the winter, I feel all's well in the world, even when it's not."

Hilda hiccuped. And still sitting, she sort of threw herself at Kata and attempted to hug her.

Kata screwed up her eyes and shrugged her off. "Leave me alone," she cried. "I mean..."

"No," wailed Hilda.

"You don't understand."

"I do! I do!" cried Hilda.

Then Kata reached out for her and took her into her

arms. "I know," she said quietly. "Hilda, you want the best – for me, for yourself. You'll be the best wife any girl could be."

"Wife!" exclaimed Mattie. "Why not woman?"

"Wife and woman," said Kata, smiling through her tears.

"It's always men men men," Mattie complained.

"When we were growing up," Ellette told Kata, "I always wished you were my sister. I don't know how to say it but, well, you're everything I'm not. So brave and strong-willed and playful and…"

This made Kata begin to weep again, and May reached out for Ellette.

"It's true, though," said Ellette. "The only thing pretty about me is my name."

"That's not what we think," May consoled her. "And Bliss – that's such a pretty name too."

Orva sat very still, as if she were line fishing from a riverbank.

Silence.

Another gaggle of pink-footed geese flew in. When she looked up at them, Kata saw one goose was struggling to keep up, and several others had fallen back to keep her company.

Orva cleared her throat.

"I agree!" she said loudly.

Everyone stared at her.

"Agree!" exclaimed Mattie. "What with, Orva?"

"Everything!" Orva said stoutly, and all the women laughed.

How dear she is, thought Kata. She's glad that we women, every woman in the village, are here together. And so am I.

"What about you, Kendra?" asked Mattie. "Do you agree with everything?"

She made a face, and everyone laughed again.

The wise woman slowly rocked to and fro. "Women are more powerful than men," she said quietly. "We can sense things. Men have to think and work them out." Kendra scratched the earth with her stick.

"It's like Kata says," Orva exclaimed. "All the boys along the Ouse are lumps and loaves!"

Everyone looked at her, astonished. They'd never heard her string so many words together.

"But you know the story of Adam," Kendra went on. "Adam and Eve. We're human beings. Women are women and men are men, and we can't escape who we are."

"What do you mean?" Ellette asked her.

That's right, thought Kata. So we have to make the best of who we're born to be. We have to make the best of who we are.

"There's an old poem," said Kendra. "It's about how we were born to suffer, and it tells us how nothing is ever easy on earth, but what it doesn't say is how we women can redeem it."

"What's redeem?" asked Orva.

"How we can save it," said Kendra. "How we women can save everyone and, well, sort of heal the world with the better part of ourselves. The part that loves, and is kind and strong, and wants peace."

All the women softly murmured in agreement.

I believe that, thought Kata. And so did my mother.

"What I'm saying," Kendra went on, "well, what I think

I want to say is that without women, quite soon there wouldn't be people. There wouldn't be children, and men would fight. So the world would come to an end, wouldn't it?" She paused. "Well, it would, wouldn't it?"

The women nodded, and Kata hugged herself, and bowed her head.

"We women have many powers. But because men are stronger – because they have stronger bodies – they often get their way. Think of us now, the English, the Vikings. At loggerheads. Fighting. But whoever wins, we all lose."

Her head still bowed, Kata's eyes filled with tears again.

Powers, she thought, and slowly she shook her head. I've got no powers.

CHAPTER 33

It was mid-afternoon, and the late September sun had crossed well into the western quarter of the sky. It had been more than two hours since Hardrada's men rode back to Eystein Orri and Young Olaf. "If we can hold on for an hour, just an hour longer," Hardrada said, "all my men in Riccall will get here."

But the English army – Earl Morcar's men, King Harold's men – kept charging at the circle of Vikings and picking them off, one by one.

Tor stood between his father and Tostig inside the circle. There are so many of them so close to me, he thought. I know they're guarding me, but I wish I could just … just break out. He stretched out both his arms in front of him, and sideways, and realized he was panting.

Then he closed his eyes and tried to pray, but he kept thinking about Kata, and how she had looked when he first saw her, at the watermill, and running along the river path in York towards *Mævill*, and when they were alone together in the stone hut, and…

In the quickening breeze, Land Ravager snapped above his head, and its dark shadow kept sweeping through him.

"That was a long prayer," said Hardrada.

Tor slowly shook his head.

"If it was a prayer," Tostig added. "Was it, Tor?"

Tor drew his shoulders together. His breathing was jerky.

Then Hardrada laid down one of his two battleaxes and clamped his large left hand on his son's shoulder. "I know! I was like you at Stiklestad."

Tor couldn't quieten his breath.

His father dug into a pocket in his breeches and held up his right fist. "Here! Have a sniff of this."

"What is it?"

"It will quieten you," Harald said, "and it will lift your spirits. Embolden you."

Then the king looked to left and to right, and then over the top of his circle, five men deep, and filled his old lungs. "We can't hold our ground," he shouted. "We must drive them back! Drive them back. Archers! Are you ready?"

"Ready!" all the Viking archers shouted.

"Loose!" the king shouted. "Loose!"

All around Tor, there was snapping, snapping and whirling and whistling, and he tightened every muscle in his body.

Many of the arrows simply bounced off the Englishmen's armour, but a good few found soft targets – necks and wrists and calves – between helmet and mail coat, mail coat and leggings.

Godwinson's men hesitated. Then they regrouped and charged for a second time.

"Loose!" roared the old king. "Loose!"

And again the Viking archers loosed a deadly volley of arrows.

But then Tor watched an Englishman strike one of the Vikings in the shield wall with his axe, and slice off his arm at the shoulder, and another man impaled a Viking warrior with his spear.

It's ending, Tor thought. Ending. My life's ending. I'm going to die.

After the next English assault, Harald's circle was no more than a couple of men deep in some places.

"We must drive them back," shouted Tor. "Back!"

"Tor!" roared King Harald Hardrada, and the heavens heard him. "Behind me! Keep right behind me! We'll cut right through their ranks. My son! Be brave, my son!"

Hardrada burst out of the circle, glaring and howling, brandishing a two-headed battleaxe in each hand.

Godwinson's most hardened men, whose work it was to guard their king, sidestepped and swayed and ducked as they tried to get out of his father's way and escape his blows. Tor ducked as well and kept as close as he could behind him.

"My son!" Harald shouted again. "Be brave, my son!"

"Father!" cried Tor. "Father!"

An English archer took very careful aim. His arrow whirred and whistled through the bright air.

Tor saw it. He saw it pierce Hardrada in the throat.

He saw the King of Norway jerk and leap into the air,

towering above all his enemies. Then Hardrada toppled backwards. He fell back, choking, into Tor's arms.

Tor gasped and screwed up his eyes. "Sk! Sk!" he gasped. "Skiss!" Fiercely he sucked the sweet air of life into his lungs and gave a terrible sob.

Then the English warriors yelled. Shoulder to shoulder, they leapt forward.

They trampled Tor and his father underfoot, and they stabbed them both to death.

They beheaded Fridrek, Harald's flag officer.

They tore down Land Ravager.

Led by Eystein Orri, more than one thousand Vikings, all fully armed, rode on horseback and ran miles on foot from Riccall to the battlefield at Stamford.

From the top of the rise where Harald had first witnessed the size and spread of Godwinson's army, Eystein could see that only small huddles of Vikings were left standing, and there was no sign of Land Ravager, no, none at all.

He closed his eyes. He took a deep, deep breath. Then he beckoned his men to gather round him. "We've no choice," he called out as loudly as he could. "None! No choice! And you've no choice."

Silence.

"We must try to avenge our king. Our leader. Harald Hardrada. We have to avenge him, or die." Eystein took a deep breath. "You're winded, I know. You're weary, I know. You can scarcely lift your swords, your shields. But you and I, we must honour Land Ravager, we must hoist it to heaven."

Eystein Orri raised both his arms above his shining helmet.

Then the mounted Vikings rode full tilt at Godwinson's men, and the men on foot ran after them.

They retrieved Hardrada's battle banner, tattered and torn, and they hoisted it.

But groups of Englishmen singled out and circled each Viking, and one by one they chopped them down.

The sweet water meadows at Stamford were strewn with crawling men from Norway, proud Vikings panting in their death throes.

The riverbank was stained with fresh, bright blood.

For some while, Godwinson allowed his men to chase and cut down their enemies, and so did Earl Morcar and Earl Edwin. But when the king saw that even Eystein Orri, their brave young leader, had been brought down, he flung off his gauntlets.

"Enough!" he said in a hoarse voice. "Enough!"

Slowly he shook his head. He trembled.

Godwinson allowed the surviving Vikings to stumble away up the rise, and head for their ships at Riccall. And as they did, his trumpeters sounded long, wavering strains – over and over again.

And it was then, as he picked his way alone through the slaughter-mist already shrouding some of the dead and dying, that Godwinson found the body of his own brother, Tostig.

Slowly he lowered himself onto his knees.

He closed his brother's eyes and instructed four of his guards to lift his corpse, and have it carried on a cart back to York, and buried there.

The hunchback moon rode high over the battlefield. Noisy ravens and harriers and buzzards and huge sea eagles gorged on the dead men's bodies and drank their blood.

CHAPTER 34

"Whoever wins, we all lose…"

Kata kept hearing the wise woman's words long after the village women had made their way back up to Poorhoe.

To begin with, she traipsed after them, but then she turned back, and thought she would stay in the stone hut in case Tor were to come back to the village early. She felt so troubled.

What if Earl Morcar plays King Harald false? Can Hardrada trust the English hostages? What if Tostig…? Will Tor have a proper horse, and where will he get armour from? What if…? I mean…

Kata was so anxious, so restless, that she jumped up and walked away from her hut again.

The moon, he told her nothing.

The stars, nothing.

The silence, nothing.

In the last watch of that late September night, the dark sky in the east started somehow to fade, and all but the brightest stars dimmed and vanished. At dawn the sky was grey and greenish, and then pale grey-blue, and the long, silent hours following it began to tell her everything she didn't want to hear.

Somewhat before midday, a horseman waving an English banner galloped straight past Kata's hut, and up the track to Poorhoe.

He kept blowing short joyous blasts on his bugle to summon the villagers, and at once shouted the news that none of them had dreamed of hearing – news that, with day after day of forced marches, Godwinson's army had reached York with bewildering speed – had reached York just in time to follow Earl Morcar to Stamford Bridge, not to exchange hostages but to confront and fight Harald Hardrada.

Kata could make out the sounds of cheering, hooting, hurrahing, and then she heard the old church bell began to ring in excited double thuds as quick as heartbeats.

Time passed.

Kata stood alone at the doorway of her stone hut, almost motionless. She gazed down the slope to where Tor had raised one hand and waved as he cantered away. Away and towards Riccall. The river. The reed beds. The waterlilies her mother loved and remembered even when she was so far from home.

When at last she turned back towards Poorhoe, she saw that the headman was plodding down the track towards her.

"Kendra said I'd likely find you here," Wilf began. "She said she came down last afternoon, and all the women with her."

Then the headman told her.

King Harold Godwinson and his army…

Harald Hardrada, King of Norway, dead.

Earl Tostig dead.

Hardrada's son dead.

"Young Olaf," said Kata.

Wilf paused. He stared at Kata. "No," he said slowly, and he sucked his cheeks. "Olaf stayed to guard the ships. At Riccall."

Kata frowned. "His son? What? What do you mean?"

Then Wilf embraced her.

"Tor," he told her. "Tor was Hardrada's son."

"Tor!"

The headman closed his eyes. "I didn't know," he murmured. "I didn't. None of us did. Not until now. That messenger…"

Kata bowed her head. She started to shake from top to toe. Bitterly she wept.

Furious, scalding, everything tears.

For herself, for Tor, for all the unending pain on this Middle Earth.

Wilf sniffed, and he shuffled a couple of steps backwards, and then sideways.

He rubbed his grey beard and worked his fingers through it.

"Your friends…" he began at last, "your friends, they'll say that we're rid of the Vikings once and for all. They'll say good riddance to Earl Tostig. They'll sing and shout that at last England is one country with one king."

Wilf took Kata's limp, warm left hand.

"But me," he went on, "I'm headman of Riccall. My flock of nineteen people. Our lives have been upended. Very likely our homes have been wrecked. And very likely there'll be too little grain in the great barn to last us through the winter. It's my duty to right things as best I can ... but I know, I well know, some things can never be righted... Only time can heal them."

Wilf fell quiet, and Kata began to sob again.

"Most likely," said the headman, "you'll want to be on your own for a while."

He reached up and pulled at a string of the creeper growing on the wall of the stone hut. The rims of its perfect little new leaves were pink, but the older leaves were jaundiced. Some of them had holes in them, and you could see all their veins.

"Our world, it's in God's hands," Wilf said, and he gave a long sigh. "Nothing's ever easy in the kingdom of earth."

Kata shuddered.

"But I'll tell you this, girl. When you do come back – when you're ready to come back – there's not one person who won't be glad of it. Not one." Gently he let go of Kata's soft hand and gripped her right shoulder. "And something else. In three days, it should be safe to go home. Back down to Riccall. That's what Godwinson's messenger told us. By then, the Viking warships, they'll have gone."

Kata looked at Wilf, wide-eyed, as if it were all too much to take in.

"Not that they'll be needing many," added Wilf. Again, he took Kata's left hand. "You're the heartbeat of our Riccall.

You know that, don't you? We can't be losing you to York and those nuns, or any such thing, if that's what you're thinking."

Over thistles and gristly roots and outcrops, she stumbled.

She knew she wasn't walking in a straight line.

My bones and everything feel all weak. They don't fit properly together.

My heart hurts.

My thoughts … they won't join up.

Without knowing where she was heading, Kata strayed towards the lonely higher hills, north from Poorhoe.

That night, she slept in a kind of earth cave, a hollow under an overhanging rock. She curled up like a red squirrel, well out of the wind, and didn't wake until dawn.

The morning was so bleak. So chill. The wind streamed down from the north, and even worked its way inside Tor's sea coat. Kata slapped her body all over to get her blood on the move again, and she chewed blades of grass. But almost as soon as she started walking, she tripped and grazed both her knees.

That day was the worst day.

Kata thought and wept and wept and remembered. Their talk, their laughter, their high hopes, their half-plans, their feelings, their precious hours together.

How long? she asked herself. How long? All in thirteen days.

Early in the afternoon, Kata came across a little grove with three wild plum trees and a generous spread of brambles. And it was only when she saw them that she realized how hungry she was. Ravenous!

She tore at the blackberries, and their spiked twigs tore at her, and bloodied her hands and arms. She picked the flesh-pink plums and stuffed her mouth with them.

Kata's face and neck and hands, her arms – they were all pinked and purpled with sticky blood and blackberry-and-plum juice.

On she walked. On and on. And quite late that afternoon, Kata saw ahead of her white smoke rising. Where is it? she wondered. Where am I?

Then she slowly realized that without meaning to, she had wheeled round in a great circle – a circle of numbness and anguish, a circle of passion and sorrow – and come back to Poorhoe.

Through several thatches, the sweet smoke lifted, lifted, and somehow Kata's heart lifted just a little with it.

Then Kata saw three small figures were charging towards her, yelling. Hurtling towards her, yelling and caterwauling.

Eager and Isen and Bliss mobbed her.

"Kata! Kata!"

"Where have you been?"

"Your face and everything."

"Red and blue."

"We've looked everywhere."

"We went down to your secret hut."

"Everyone's looking."

"Where have you been?"

Kata shook her tangled hair and combed it backwards between her stained fingers, and here and there a twisted strand shone in the late sunlight.

"Away," she told them. "So far away."

Eager and Isen tugged at Tor's lumpen sea coat, and little Bliss wrapped her arms around Kata's legs.

"Off with you now!" Kata begged them. "Tell everyone you've found me. Tell them I've been far away. I'll come after you."

Away they ran, the three of them, and after a while a feeling crept into Kata's strong heart. At first it was floating and indefinite. But then it somehow turned into a thought in her head as well. It spoke to her, and bright blood quickened and coursed round her body.

Far away, she thought. So far away…

It's true, I could go to the nunnery. Sister Innocenta promised me. *You can always come back,* she said.

I could prepare skins and learn to read… Is that what Kendra meant when she said we all have powers? But I'd soon want to live outside as well as inside – without as well as within. I know I would.

Kata sat down on a rock and laced her fingers over her stomach.

Far away, she thought. So far away…

I could.

Couldn't I?

Tor told me that his mother and my mother were like sisters, almost.

He said I'd really like her, and I would. I know I would.

I could tell her everything.

On her farm, I could help her.

If I can sail north.

I could.

*Deadbeat. When the Vikings dipped
their oars and slipped away downriver,
they needed only seventeen ships.
They left the corpses of their companions
as a banquet for the horny-beaked raven
garbed in black, the grey-coated eagle
with its white tail, and that howling beast,
the wolf in the wood. Never once
before that day were more men slain
in battle for this – the island of England.*

ACKNOWLEDGEMENTS

This is the seventh and last of my novels set during the Middle Ages, and once again many people have helped it on its way. In particular, I thank my eagle-eyed and supportive wife, Linda, my dear friend the historian Richard Barber, and my long-time reader-cum-editor Lynda Edwardes-Evans for her detailed response to my drafts. I'm indebted to my publisher, Denise Johnstone-Burt, and to Annalie Grainger for helping me to rearrange and hasten this story, and to Meera Santiapillai and Ben Norland, my overseer and art editor at Walker Books. Karen Clarke, much-missed, first engaged with this story more than three years ago, and for more than a year now, Vikki Powles has been my highly accomplished and effervescent PA.

King Harald's Saga, translated by Magnus Magnusson and Hermann Pálsson (Penguin Books, 1966) and John Marsden's biography, *Harald Hardrada: The Warrior's Way* (Sutton, 2007), have been invaluable sources of inspiration while writing this novel.

"Spectacular and enjoyable." *Sunday Times*

The gods, led by all-powerful Odin and mighty Thor, are caught in a terrifying struggle for power with the fearsome giants. They must battle them using all their cunning and strength. But the gods' greatest enemy lurks among them: the trickster Loki.

"An absolute treasure for any age." *Daily Mail*

Enter the enthralling world of Arthurian legend: the timeless tales of the sword in the stone, the knights of the Round Table, the magic of Merlin and the betrayal of Lancelot and Guinevere are brought to life in this lyrical and lavishly illustrated edition.

"An incredible tale." *WRD Magazine*

Wulfstan, an intrepid sailor, dazzles King Alfred the Great and his court with his account of a shipwreck, a thrilling horse race and a dead king buried in an ice coffin.

Kevin Crossley-Holland has won the Carnegie Medal and the Guardian Children's Fiction Prize, and is also an acclaimed poet and translator of *Beowulf* from Anglo-Saxon. His Arthur trilogy attracted worldwide critical praise, sold well over one million copies and has been translated into twenty-five languages. A recognized expert on folklore and Norse mythology, his most recent work includes *Norse Myths*, *Between Worlds: Folktales of Britain & Ireland* and *Arthur: The Always King*, spectacularly illustrated by Chris Riddell.

Kevin was president of the School Library Association 2012–2017 and has been awarded honorary doctorates by Anglia Ruskin and Worcester universities. He is a Fellow of the Royal Society of Literature and the Society of Authors, and patron of the Society for Storytelling and the Story Museum. He now lives with his Minnesotan wife in Norfolk and he has four children and nine grandchildren.